T0340319

The Morality of Economic Behaviour

The links between self-interest and morality have been examined in moral philosophy since Plato. Economics is a mostly value-free discipline, having lost its original ethical dimension as described by Adam Smith. Examining moral philosophy through the framework provided by economics offers new insights into both disciplines and the discussion on the origins and nature of morality.

The Morality of Economic Behaviour: Economics as Ethics argues that moral behaviour does not need to be exogenously encouraged or enforced because morality is a side effect of interactions between self-interested agents. The argument relies on two important parameters: behaviour in a social environment and the effects of intertemporal choice on rational behaviour. Considering social structures and repeated interactions on rational maximisation allows an argument for the morality of economic behaviour. Amoral agents interacting within society can reach moral outcomes. Thus, economics becomes a synthesis of moral and rational choice theory bypassing the problems of ethics in economic behaviour whilst promoting moral behaviour and ethical outcomes. This approach sheds new light on practical issues such as economic policy, business ethics and social responsibility.

This book is of interest primarily to students of politics, economics and philosophy but will also appeal to anyone who is interested in morality and ethics, and their relationship with self-interest.

Vangelis Chiotis is a Lecturer at Glasgow Caledonian University, UK.

Routledge INEM Advances in Economic Methodology
Series Editor: Esther-Mirjam Sent, the University of Nijmegen, the Netherlands.

The field of economic methodology has expanded rapidly during the last few decades. This expansion has occurred in part because of changes within the discipline of economics, in part because of changes in the prevailing philosophical conception of scientific knowledge, and also because of various transformations within the wider society. Research in economic methodology now reflects not only developments in contemporary economic theory, the history of economic thought, and the philosophy of science; but it also reflects developments in science studies, historical epistemology, and social theorizing more generally. The field of economic methodology still includes the search for rules for the proper conduct of economic science, but it also covers a vast array of other subjects and accommodates a variety of different approaches to those subjects.

The objective of this series is to provide a forum for the publication of significant works in the growing field of economic methodology. Since the series defines methodology quite broadly, it will publish books on a wide range of different methodological subjects. The series is also open to a variety of different types of works: original research monographs, edited collections, as well as republication of significant earlier contributions to the methodological literature. The International Network for Economic Methodology (INEM) is proud to sponsor this important series of contributions to the methodological literature.

The Philosophy of Causality in Economics
Causal Inferences and Policy Proposals
Mariusz Maziarz

The Morality of Economic Behaviour
Economics as Ethics
Vangelis Chiotis

For more information about this series, please visit: www.routledge.com/Routledge-INEM-Advances-in-Economic-Methodology/book-series/SE0630

The Morality of Economic Behaviour

Economics as Ethics

Vangelis Chiotis

Routledge
Taylor & Francis Group

LONDON AND NEW YORK

First published 2021
by Routledge
2 Park Square, Milton Park, Abingdon, Oxon OX14 4RN

and by Routledge
605 Third Avenue, New York, NY 10017

First issued in paperback 2022

Routledge is an imprint of the Taylor & Francis Group, an informa business

© 2021 Vangelis Chiotis

The right of Vangelis Chiotis to be identified as author of this work
has been asserted by him in accordance with sections 77 and 78 of the
Copyright, Designs and Patents Act 1988.

All rights reserved. No part of this book may be reprinted or
reproduced or utilised in any form or by any electronic, mechanical,
or other means, now known or hereafter invented, including
photocopying and recording, or in any information storage or
retrieval system, without permission in writing from the publishers.

Trademark notice: Product or corporate names may be trademarks
or registered trademarks, and are used only for identification and
explanation without intent to infringe.

Publisher's Note
The publisher has gone to great lengths to ensure the quality of this
reprint but points out that some imperfections in the original copies
may be apparent.

British Library Cataloguing-in-Publication Data
A catalogue record for this book is available from the British Library

Library of Congress Cataloging-in-Publication Data
Names: Chiotis, Vangelis, author.
Title: The morality of economic behaviour: economics as
ethics / Vangelis Chiotis.
Description: 1 Edition. | New York: Routledge, 2020. |
Series: Routledge inem advances in economic methodology |
Includes bibliographical references and index.
Identifiers: LCCN 2020007725 (print) | LCCN 2020007726 (ebook)
Subjects: LCSH: Economics—Moral and ethical aspects. |
Ethics—Economic aspects. | Rational choice theory.
Classification: LCC HB72 .C465 2020 (print) | LCC HB72 (ebook) |
DDC 174/.4—dc23
LC record available at https://lccn.loc.gov/2020007725
LC ebook record available at https://lccn.loc.gov/2020007726

ISBN 13: 978-0-367-50762-6 (pbk)
ISBN 13: 978-0-8153-4773-6 (hbk)
ISBN 13: 978-1-351-16888-5 (ebk)

DOI: 10.4324/9781351168885

Typeset in Times New Roman
by codeMantra

Contents

1 Introduction

Morality is usually seen as a constraint on self-interested maximisation and economic behaviour. This book argues that morality is a side effect of interactions between self-interested agents. As a result, economic behaviour does not need constraints in order to be ethical, and moral behaviour does not need to be exogenously encouraged or enforced. This argument is different from most of the literature in economic philosophy and ethics, which focus on constraining economic maximisation to ensure ethical outcomes and the potential ethical implications of economic policies. The links between rationality and morality have been examined in political philosophy at least since Plato. However, economics, especially in the last century, has become value-free losing its original ethical dimension as described by Adam Smith. Robert Reich in his *Saving Capitalism* makes a similar point; in criticising free market he says "if you're not paid enough to live on, so be it" (Reich, 2017: 1). His argument is more practice orientated than the one proposed here, but the aim is similar: a restatement of capitalism. In a similar vein, Frank (1988) examines the links between emotions and rationality and addresses the 'commitment problem', which poses problems for rational interactions, through an appeal to non-exclusively rational motives. Sandel argues for moral limits on markets, explaining that market outcomes will otherwise be unethical (Sandel, 2012). However, the argument made here starts from individual maximisation and argues for greater freedom for markets, given certain conditions that will lead to market optimisation. Paul Bloom makes an argument for reason and rationality and against empathy (2018). The present argument is similar in that rationality is seen a better way to deal with moral issues.

Economic behaviour here has two meanings. First, rational, self-interested behaviour as prescribed by mainstream economic theory. Second, the behaviour in the real world economic marketplace.

Free market capitalism is very much alive and well, but it has failed a big part of the world in wealthy and developing societies. The problem is popularly highlighted by events such as the 2008 financial crisis and phenomena such as the increasing wealth inequality. The reduction of global extreme poverty is not such a popular topic (Rosling, 2019), but it is very much true. So, free market capitalism still works – sometimes. Here, I wish to take issue with the times that it does not work, namely cases where free market outcomes are morally indefensible by anyone. In doing so I propose a qualification of rational, economic behaviour and an account of minimal morality.

The argument relies on two important parameters: collective action and the effects of intertemporal choice on rational choice (Ostrom, 2000). Considering social structures and repeated interactions on rational maximisation, allows an argument for the morality of economic behaviour. Amoral agents interacting within society can reach moral outcomes. Thus, economics becomes a synthesis of moral and rational choice theory bypassing the problems of ethics in economic behaviour whilst promoting moral behaviour and ethical outcomes. This approach sheds new light on practical issues such as economic policy, business ethics and social responsibility.

Chapter 1 introduces the debate on social morality and argues for the need for a rationality-based theory of morality. Considering the impact of social interactions on rational agency and behaviour, allows arguing for rational morality, the idea that moral behaviour stems from self-interest. The chapter explains how rational morality, which is primarily investigated by political and moral philosophy, is related to economic theory. Moral behaviour is taken to be a synthesis of ideas introduced by Hume and Hobbes in that it requires rationality and sociability; social conventions, as the result of repeated interactions between rational agents, serve as enforcement mechanism, ensuring maximisation within social constraints and through behaviour that can be characterised as moral. Morality is then not externally imposed, but a pre-condition for maximisation. This stands in opposition to Kantian and to an extent Rawlsian approaches to morality and justice. In both contemporary economic theory and political philosophy there is an implicit social contract that regulates behaviour (Forst, 2002; Cudd, 2007). Contractarianism, broadly understood, can be used to examine both economics and morality. Proponents of the efficiency of free markets accept the idea that mutual advantage is adequate to regulate behaviour in the same way that political and moral contractarians accept that an appeal to reason is sufficient for the establishment of a social contract. The argument presented in the chapter and by extension the book, is that contractarianism can offer valuable insights about economic theory, free market operations and the morality of economic activities.

Economic rationality is qualified so that it fits in the social approach taken. This is similar to sociological discussions of rational agency; however, it is done in the context of morality, not just social interactions. Morality, ethics and justice are discussed in terms of economic theory and practice. The three concepts are interlinked but separate; moral behaviour leads to just outcomes, whereas ethics describes the socially acceptable norms of behaviour. Economic maximisation is a social activity and as such, relies on and is influenced by others. The idea that all interactions are strategic and repeated allows for the introduction of other-regarding motives in rational deliberation and therefore, the inclusion of morality. An implication of the synthesis between rational and moral behaviour is that immorality must be rooted in irrationality, given the social nature of rationality presented here. Moreover, given the approach taken here morality is not to be forced upon people's behaviour and as a result, immoral outcomes are possible. Ultimately, the chapter examines whether economics is an immoral, an amoral or a moral discipline.

The second chapter looks at how economic theory and the assumption of self-interested behaviour can have moral implications. In *The Theory of Moral Sentiments* Smith argues that humans show, or should show, sympathy to one another, like an impartial spectator would – similarly to Harsanyi's impartial observer and Rawls's ideal observer (Binmore, 1989). Hence, there can be a hypothetical, asocial person who can be impartial and dictate moral behaviour. Moral agents have to think from the perspective of the impartial spectator in order to decide whether an act is moral or not. The *Wealth of Nations* is about the market economy and as a result and to an extent, about self-interested, as opposed to moral behaviour. The idea of the impartial spectator is replaced in terms of importance by the concept of the invisible hand. Although the phrase itself is only used once in the book, it is indicative of Smith's understanding of how markets work. The free market mechanism, nationally or internationally, is automatic and advantageous for participants when left to operate freely.

Therefore, on one hand Smith's moral theory can be seen as paternalistic in that it requires someone better informed and above society to decide what is moral. On the other hand his economic theory, allows for anarchic interpretations of the economy. However, this is not necessarily true on two accounts. First, Smith's work as a whole is an argument for individual freedom. His moral theory is an argument for freedom from religion (Heilbroner, 1986) or social authorities whose behaviour is not justified by the ideal spectator. Smith's economic theory is an argument for freedom from government intervention in the market place. Second, both the moral and the economic theory rely on the ability to judge and assess behaviour objectively by using impartiality and profit making respectively. One's behaviour or a given social arrangement can be assessed by reference to asocial objective rules, which must be accepted by reasonable interlocutors.

The objection to this interpretation of Smith might be that his moral theory calls for altruistic behaviour, whereas his economic theory calls for egoism. However, Smith understands free market as a mechanism for profit through mutual advantage and hence, being egoistic has a positive impacts on others. If there can be no mutual advantage there can be no market. In the absence of the conditions necessary to form a market, behaviour as dictated by the ideal spectator takes over. Self and other-regarding behaviour rely on different motivations, but they are very similar expressively. The two types of behaviour as presented by Smith, complement each other and highlight how Smith and economic theory can be included in the contractarian paradigm and the idea of mutual advantage as the cornerstone for rational and moral behaviour.

Chapter 3 turns to sociability. For Adam Smith, individuals operate within a society and therefore, they are influenced by others and by social norms. However, for most of mainstream economic theory, the impact of society on individual behaviour is not examined. Therefore, examining how social structures affect rational maximisation will provide a link between the roots of economic theory and its contemporary understanding. The chapter examines the impact of social structures on individual rational choice. The argument is that an action that is deemed rational for an isolated Robinson Crusoe is not necessarily rational for an economic agent who operates in a society (Grapard and Hewitson, 2012). All interactions take place in a social context and as such, are iterated. As a result, interactions represented by the Prisoner's Dilemma (PD) game are maximising when they are cooperative. An adjusted version of the game that considers the impact of sociability is more appropriate and can offer more useful insights. Sociability proves to be the link between moral and rational behaviour, in the vein of Adam Smith's work but more explicitly and using a game theoretical framework to examine interactions.

In this understanding cooperation in the PD game is very close to morality (Taylor, 1987). However, there is one fundamental difference; cooperation refers to interlocutors in a one-off interaction or a series of interactions. Morality on the other hand, refers to internalising and expressing cooperative behaviour throughout one's interactions within society and punishing defectors. Given repeated interactions within a given social structure, one cooperates by default and without expecting cooperative behaviour in return by the given interlocutor. Whereas cooperation is a strategy that can be adopted reciprocally, morality is a type of behaviour that is adopted throughout one's life interactions. In the proposed understanding, moral behaviour is not necessarily cooperation in a PD game. Moral behaviour is dictated by the established social equilibrium and given repeated interactions and information availability the efficient social equilibrium, which ensures individual utility maximisation, must be a cooperative one. Given time and information, we should expect that social equilibria are Pareto optimal, but rational morality can only ensure efficiency. As such, we will have to agree that an established social status that is accepted by free individuals meets rational morality criteria. As with the case of cooperation and morality, the outcome of rational agents interacting over time must be Pareto optimal and thus, moral.

As a consequence of repeated interactions within a social context, intertemporal choice is the focus of Chapter 4. Rational agents have to consider time, as well as interlocutors' strategies over time, in adopting maximising strategies. This chapter draws from the literature on dynamic choice and rationality. In a social setting rational agents very rarely have to make decisions in a static environment; the number and disposition of potential interlocutors may change and other parameters affecting one's decision are also subject to change. Therefore, an account of dynamic rationality is needed in order to examine rational agency and decision-making over time. Rationality over the long term is linked to sociability and social rationality and the rational justifiability of other-regarding behaviour. Economic accounts of rational agency will not allow maximisation over a series of interactions. However, assuming that economic agents are time conscious allows interactions without immediate maximisation, and as a result allows for behaviour that can be characterised as moral.

Chapter 5 examines information availability as a consequence of sociability and intertemporality. Information availability is essential for rational behaviour. Within societies or social groups experience of previous interactions becomes common knowledge and therefore, rational agents adopt similar strategies as they have similar experiences and access to similar information. The basis of this understanding is that behavioural equilibria are the result of information availability. In turn, these equilibria of social behaviour are structurally similar to social conventions. The discussion on information availability includes an examination of rational agency and social conventions, and the impact that information availability has on rationality and the stability of social conventions. Information equality is the result of social interaction within social structures that preserve memory of past interaction and promote maximising behaviour.

The concluding chapter examines the implications of the theoretical argument of the first five chapters for real world interactions. Business ethics, ethical boycotting, the internet as information spreading mechanism, the shared economy, financial ethics and micro-finance, are some of the economic phenomena that can be seen to achieve economic success as well as moral outcomes. Moreover, there are other areas of economic activity such as labour relations, financial and supra-national corporations, the food industry, where the ethical dimension of supply and distribution have been the focus of attention and public debate. Economics as an ethical theory shows that efficiency in economic terms must correspond to ideas of justice as mutual advantage and that profit maximising behaviour corresponds to moral behaviour. In order for this argument to hold then we need to revisit the idea of free markets and capitalism and base it on the ideas of Adam Smith who argued for a mutual advantage capitalism in opposition to the current model of financial and corporate capitalism. This is an alternative approach to free market capitalism and answers contemporary anti-capitalistic criticism.

The financial crisis of 2008 for example was the result of individuals and corporations maximising profit at the expense of their 'customers', taking advantage of information and power asymmetries. Chapter 2 argues for an understanding of Smith's work that incorporates moral, economic and social behaviour, whereas modern capitalism relies on keeping these realms separate. At the same time, the argument presented here is one for freedom of markets, as identified in Smith's work, which relies on freedom and responsibility of individuals. Repeated interactions between informed individuals lead to social equilibria that are efficient and moral. Individual freedom and responsibility, as well as the sustainability and efficiency of social equilibria all rely on information availability, within a given society. Theoretically information availability, and even information equality, is ensured by the assumption of repeated interactions. As interaction history develops within a social group or society, its members develop a better understanding of how potential interlocutors are likely to behave in the future, using past behaviour as basis for prediction. Practically, this is not as straightforward; however, information today is much more easily spread than a few years ago thanks to technological advancements. Assuming access to the internet for instance, it is plausible to assert that all consumers have access to the same information about a certain product. It is then their personal responsibility to decide whether they should consume it. For example, everyone has the capacity to know whether an investment portfolio relies on high risk investments, which food is organic, a given bank executives' salaries. It is up to the individual consumer to decide whether she ought to consume the given product. As such, information symmetries in the market place are more plausible today than even before, mostly because of advancements in information technology. They are not always present, information symmetries in the sense of information equality within the bounds of a society is a possibility and present in many cases. As a result, social equilibria that regulate and promote moral behaviour, as discussed in earlier chapters, can become established. In this context, social equilibria that call for risky investments or industrially produced food can also become established, but they cannot be as efficient as equilibria that rely on long-term sustainability.

2 Rational morality in economics

Economic theory relies on the concept of homo-economicus, the idea that economic agents are self-interested and rational. Economic practice is about people as they are, rather than how they might be. Other-regarding, altruistic behaviour is impossible in the former case and rare in the latter. The literature on economics and morality focuses on constraints on economic behaviour, with Sandel's and Bowles's work being characteristic of the approach (Bowles and Gintis, 2013). The argument proposed here is that economic, self-interested behaviour can lead to moral outcomes, without external constraints to individual maximisation. In the proposed account, economics serves as a framework for a theory of moral behaviour, rather than assume that economic and moral behaviour are opposites. As such, the argument is similar to Broome's (1999) but the focus here is normative not methodological, relying on assumption of rational agency and the importance of social interactions. Sen's approach to economics and justice (1988, 2009) takes a different path in arguing for justice but again the currently proposed argument relies on rational agency rather than reasonable agreement.

The model of homo-economicus defines economic theory and the debate about the nature and limits of personal responsibility is central to moral philosophy. The individual, her environment and the interplay between the two can be used to examine how economics can serve as an instrument for morality. When the root moral behaviour is accepted to be the individual, economics can be used as an analytical tool to better understand moral behaviour. Economics is shown to be the study of morals as much as it is a discipline examining profit making and rational choice.

In addition to the potential moral outcomes of economic behaviour, it can be shown that economics is an intrinsic part of the social sciences with direct implications for assumptions of individuality and individual behaviour in economics. Hence, the focus shifts to social interactions broadly, not exclusively economic interactions aiming at profit or utility maximisation. The starting is economic, self-interested behaviour which is filtered through social interactions to lead to moral outcomes. Economics is the toolbox for a moral argument that relies on self-interest and, as a result, is more powerful than theories of ethics that rely on individuals following moral rules or exogenous constraints on individual behaviour.

The ethical theory proposed has its roots in economic theory thinking but it also has direct implications for economic theory, practice and the operation of free market. Economic theory relies on the idea that market competition leads to mutually advantageous outcomes. This assumes that free interactions are possible and beneficial, for both the individual and society. However, the theory of free market interactions ignores power asymmetries. It does not consider the possibility that one party might be so much stronger than the others that mutually beneficial interaction becomes difficult and requires altruistic motives. In exclusively economic terms, monopolies are seen as threat to free markets, the same way that power discrepancies are a threat to mutually beneficial interactions among rational interlocutors. The discussion here is not just about strictly economic monopolies but also about the underlying premise in contemporary capitalism that 'bigger is better'. Economic practice, unlike much of mainstream economic theory, is full of examples of corporations that are too big to be regulated. In economic theory, government intervenes to ensure that free market interactions lead to utility and welfare maximisation.

However, this is not always the case in practice – or even, it is seldom the case in practice. The power discrepancies that exist between consumers and corporations, also arise between corporations and governments and between firms of different sizes. Although arguably the latter two are not as extreme as the former, they are still present and significant enough to make a difference in market operations and lead to what in economic theory is called 'market failure'. Market power discrepancies such as these are the result of institutional failure in the sense that corporations have been allowed to become oversized by government intervention failures – they are in many respects institutionally supported. This type of market failure, supported or at least allowed by governments and their institutions, is not always recognised as such precisely because market failures are defined by governments (North, 1991). As a result, capitalism and free market fail much more frequently that economic theory predicts and economic practice admits. The proposed solution is imposing limits on such concentration of power. However, unlike mainstream economic theory the limits are not imposed and enforced by governments, which has proven inefficient in doing so, especially in recent years. The proposed account argues for limits against extreme power and market inefficiencies that are endogenous and stem from individual rationality and individual responsibility. Rational agents must choose to avoid such power inequalities which lead to a bottom-up capitalistic market that is defined by interactions between rational economic agents – similar to capitalism as described by Adam Smith.

In its theoretical form, market competition is not in conflict with morality or ethics, broadly understood. Economic agents interact freely aiming to make profit, which also leads to increasing social welfare. As such, economic theory has moral implications in that economic interactions are mutually beneficial and therefore, fair. Consumers interact with bakers and butchers for mutual benefit. Neither party is assumed or expected to behave morally but the outcome of their interactions is moral because it is mutually beneficial, without harm for any part. Should one of the parties not think so, they can change their behaviour and avoid further interactions – there're always other bakeries around. This is not the case in contemporary markets, where corporations have created information monopolies and have gathered too much power for the market to be competitive. As a result, the interaction between a consumer and a supplier is characterised by significant and extreme power discrepancies, in a way that corrupts free market. In addition, information asymmetries and misinformation violate one of the fundamental premises of free market interaction. Markets cannot possibly lead to efficient outcomes because they are no longer free (Hausman, 1989).

Bottom-up capitalism

Economics, capitalism and morality have the same roots, namely rationality. It can be shown that self-interested individuals have reasons to be prudent when deliberating on a strategy. This does not entail forfeiting on their own benefit and individual utility maximisation; rather the argument is that interactions among self-interested individuals have outcomes that can be seen as other-regarding or moral. Self-interested behaviour has positive externalities. As a consequence, capitalism can work efficiently yielding profits if rational agency is its building block. An example can better explain part of the problem and the proposed solution; Google has been a company of technological innovation, among other things. Becoming a public company has shifted its focus from innovating to generating profits for its share-holders. The two should be linked; innovative products that are popular with consumers should lead to profits for the company. However, beneficial results from innovation, and production, take time to realise, whereas financial gains from tax schemes for example can be seen on yearly basis, if not shorter periods. There is, for Google and other similar companies, a disconnect between what they do as companies, producing popular goods, and their profitability. As such, the current version of capitalism does not work without corporate and financial capitalism; a successful firm is expected to expand and issue shares in order to compete, which in turn makes its operations corrupted by the need for positive financial results, not exclusively positive market results. The difference between the two might seem fine but it is not; a firm's success, even financial success, can be driven by its products' popularity or its financial competency. When it is the latter we can talk about corporate or financial capitalism, which is a corrosive force in free-market capitalism as it facilitates a disconnect between what a firm produces and its profits. Contemporary capitalism is too centralised and power asymmetrical to operate as capitalism was meant to – a system of free interactions between rational maximisers that leads to mutual benefit. The argument itself is not new, although it has been becoming increasingly popular. Wofl spoke of 'rigged capitalism', explaining that capitalism does not work any more – or at least that finance has corrupted capitalism. Similarly, publicly traded firms are not ran by their shareholders but by boards aiming to maximise shareholders profile, whilst ignoring long-term economic viability.

The ultimate goal is to re-examine and re-evaluate capitalism as it has developed in recent decades, with special focus on corporate capitalism. This is to be achieved through a re-evaluation of the premises of economic theory with clear implications for economic practice. Capitalism is far from dead, but there is a need to re-establish it as the means and the framework for social interactions that lead to mutually advantageous outcomes, including profit. Corporate capitalism relies on power asymmetries and fails to achieve mutual benefit. As such, it cannot be sustainable. Highlighting the conceptual links between moral behaviour and economic activity within the freedom afforded by theoretical capitalism can show that capitalism not only can lead to moral outcome but that it must do so in order to work. To achieve this, a discussion of the fundamentals of rational agency and moral behaviour is in order, which should show how the two can be reconciled. Rational morality, the idea that morality can be rooted in rationality, is a concept used in moral and political philosophy, but paradoxically not in economics. Its absence from economic theory is paradoxical and significant because mainstream economic theory although focusing primarily on market interactions, utility maximisation and profit making is not indifferent to the potential outcomes of rational interactions.

Morality is seen here to be the result of interactions between rational agents, with society acting as the transformative filter. Economic theory is born out of assumptions of self-interest and rationality, which may lead to social welfare (Hargreaves-Heap, 1989). Qualified definitions of rational and moral behaviour will allow making an argument about how interactions among self-interested, economic agents lead to a moral outcome. The qualified definition of rational behaviour is influenced by institutional, behavioural economics. As such, although not part of mainstream economic theory they are also not completely independent from economic thinking. In addition, the qualified definition for rational agency is influenced by economics as introduced my Adam Smith; a discipline about society and social behaviour as well as production and market operations.

The basis for the proposed argument is three-fold: First, examine the roots of morality and the extent to which these can be traced to rationality and self-interested behaviour. Second, examine the viability and sustainability of the current version of capitalism and third, argue for the morality of free-market capitalism. The argument lies on the premise that the idea of free market and free market interactions ensure individual freedom and thus, they are an essential characteristic of a moral interaction within a liberal framework where individual liberty is an essential condition (Narveson and Dimock, 2000). In addition, the argument made here relies on an account of rational agency that highlights the influence of social dynamics on individual behaviour and rationality. As such, socially rational agents interacting freely within a market reach outcomes that are moral.

These three things are elements of a critique of corporate capitalism, which relies on power asymmetries. The critique is based on a theoretical framework of moral philosophy and philosophy of economics. As such, the argument is primarily theoretical and normative, dealing with rational morality and issues of moral philosophy but at the same time, it has clear implications for economic theory and practice. The account is methodologically individualistic. It starts from looking at individual behaviour but it does not ignore social influence and group dynamics. Although the importance of the interdependence between the individual and the social is central to the argument, the level of analysis remains the individual, just as in mainstream economic theory. The individualistic approach is in accordance with liberal theories of morality, where individual freedom cannot be violated, when the harm principle is not violated.

Endogenous and exogenous morality

Morality and rationality are commonly thought of as opposites. One is taken to be about empathy and altruistic behaviour and the other about self-interested behaviour. However, morality can be shown to be a side-effect of self-interested behaviour. Examining moral behaviour in an economic theory framework, using analytical tools from economic theory sets the ethics bar low. Economic theory is largely amoral – and some might call its outcomes immoral. However, this is the strength of the argument. If, starting from amoral premises, morality can be reached then certainly morality can be reached when the starting point is not amoral. Assuming the worse about human behaviour included behaviour that is slightly better, adding force to the theory. If an argument for moral behaviour can be used to convince homo-economicus, or to sociopaths unable to show regard for others, then certainly the same argument will work on people who although self-interested are able to be empathetic – just like most real life people.

The current argument relies on considering the three parameters mentioned above, the discussion of each takes up one chapter. The first parameter, the idea that all human interactions take place in a social environment may sound tautological but it is a departure from the homo-economicus model that forms the basis for mainstream economic theory. Assuming sociability affects the conclusions we can draw about individual behaviour both on the rational and the moral realm. The second assumption is that time is a consideration which affects deliberation and behaviour. The impact of time is two-fold. First it influences the time-frame for decision-making; agents need to consider how their actions in the present will affect them in the future. Second, time has an impact on the individual herself, her ability for rational deliberation and the factors affecting her deliberation process; for example, and cautiously following Parfit, an agent's utility function and preferences are not constant through her life. Finally, it is assumed that interlocutors have access to the same information; for morality to be the outcome of rationality there is a need for information symmetry or at least the absence of significant information asymmetries. These three parameters complement each other and all three are essential components of the presented argument. Sociability leads to intertemporality, which ensures information symmetry.

Morality is thought to be achieved by constraints on rationality, either endogenous such as the development of 'moral character', or exogenous such as established laws and punishment by social institutions. Endogenous moral constraints, or moral behaviour that is character-based, are limited in that moral individuals can still commit immoral actions; one's character is beyond the scope of the present argument as here, we are only interested in expressive preferences and disposition to act only when it is followed by the corresponding action. Put differently, social science and social philosophy are interested in what people do and can be observed by others, not in their character or their capacity to act morally or immorally. Moreover, the reliance on moral character makes it more likely that an agent acts morally in most but not necessarily all interactions and as such, it leaves a gap in understanding and explaining what happens when he behaves immorally. Furthermore, it seems that basing an argument on the existence of moral character bypasses the problem of development of such a character and even more importantly the issue of developing and exhibiting such a character in a variety of social interactions.

Exogenous moral constraints on rational behaviour are problematic because they rely on a third party, thus shifting the issue of moral behaviour. Understanding morality as an element of rationality, bypasses the problem of enforceability. Morality based on rationality is self-imposed, assuming that actors are rational. Rational agency, being the cornerstone of economic theory, makes economic theory an ideal conceptual basis for an argument for rational morality. The second argument made here is that economics is, or at least can be interpreted as, a theory of ethics and justice; this is the case when we consider Adam Smith's work in *The Theory of Moral Sentiments and An Inquiry into the Nature and Causes of the Wealth of Nations*. Smith's work on political economy is influenced by his work on moral philosophy and the two have overlap. Hence, it is possible to interpret his work as a unified project. Both arguments, that morality must be self-imposed and that economics is a theory of justice, have practical implications about the organisation of social life, applied ethics and ultimately current economic theory application and the contemporary approaches to free market and capitalism.

Scope: ethics, morals and justice

Ethics refers to rules that dictate socially acceptable behaviour. They are rules that apply to the whole of a given society or a specific group and whose violation causes condemnation, exclusion from the group or punishment by other means (Weirich, 2011). Morals refer to rules of behaviour that apply to individuals, influenced by social rules and ethics but not determined by them (Bicchieri, 2002). Ethics then are social rules of how we ought to live, whereas morals are individual rules on how one ought to behave. Justice is the outcome of following these rules, or similarly of a society that abides by these rules. In slightly different terminology, justice is the social equilibrium that is the result of interactions among moral agents. The last sentence carries implications for the scope of justice in the current argument. Running a red light is a violation of a social and legal rule, and one should not do so. However, doing so does not constitute violation of moral rules.

Since morality is about personal rules of how one ought to behave, running a red light can be considered immoral if one is inclined to include traffic rules in the realm of morality. The expectation for others to stop at red light then, is a moral expectation if one himself stops at red lights as part of his moral deliberation. As such, the scope of morality, and ethics, can be very wide, but it is commonly more specific. For the current account and although no hard boundaries will be set, we will assume that morality has to include social interactions, not just social rules. So, one behaves immorally if one benefits from it, while harming someone else, whereas one behaves morally when one benefits himself or others, without harm being done to anyone. Therefore, morality and ethics apply exclusively to social interactions. Damaging a car cannot be considered immoral; given the social basis hurting an animal cannot be considered immoral either. However, both these statements will be qualified and analysed further when discussing sociability.

Starting from assumptions of individuality and moral separability of persons, we need to approach justice as an outcome of social interactions for mutual advantage. This is important for two reasons. First, it allows to link economic theory and an account of maximising agent, similar to homo-economicus, to ethics. Second, it offers a stronger moral theory that relies on self-interest as opposed to assumed concern for others as part of human personality or character. Assuming that selfish individuals can exhibit moral behaviour through social interactions is a stronger argument than starting from assumptions entailing a moral character. That is not to say that humans do not have a moral character. However, the emphasis here is to include even those who do not or who behave as if they do not; those with a moral disposition are also included as they meet the moral requirements, even though their motives are moral instead of rational. In a sense, we speak of expressive morality – individuals are not expected to be moral, just to act morally in a social setting. Social interaction between self-interested agents leads to social equilibria that promote and ensure moral behaviour. In addition, the current account focuses on social interactions and as such, interactions between family members, friends or partners, are not its primary focus; interactions where interlocutors are mutually-concerned, and where one's utility function may include another's benefit can be examined through the proposed rationality framework but the current argument primarily aims to convince those who behave or are disposed to behave immorally.

The assumption of self-interested behaviour expands the circle of morality by including those, no matter how many, who do not have moral, other-regarding considerations. Expanding the circle of morality is especially important for an economic approach to morality, where individuals are assumed to be self-interested. Also, it offers a more encompassing theory as it does not require agents to be reasonable, as Rawls's contractarianism, but it starts from a minimalistic approach to the essential assumptions for human behaviour. More importantly, and perhaps more realistically, it includes those whose moral reasoning differs from commonly accepted rules of morality. As such, there is one core starting assumption about individual preferences and behaviour: that individuals want to maximise their utility. This is a reductionist account of the homo-economicus model, not assuming hyper-rationality, but just mutual-unconcern.

Rational agency in context

Economic rationality ignores the importance of social interactions by assuming, and asserting, independence of utility functions. This assumption is fundamental for economic theory and its applications, especially for economic modelling. However, in its simplicity it misses an essential characteristic of human behaviour and its implications, namely social interactions.

I propose an account of rationality where individual agency interacts with social dynamics. A rational individual is taken to be a utility maximiser with a consistent order of preferences over a set of alternatives. However, the content of preferences is not examined in assessing the rationality of one's behaviour. In other words, "[w]e do not know what [the rational man] wants...but we know his indifference curves are concave to the origin." (Hollis, 1975: 75). Similarly, the behaviour of both the grasshopper and the ant are rational (Gauthier, 1986). They are both utility maximisers by being heedless and prudent respectively. Provided that imprudence is the result of reflective thinking and its long-term implications are being appreciated, then there is no reason to classify it as irrational. The choice of a 'rational' strategy depends on the parameters of a given society.

In games with the structure of a Prisoner's Dilemma (PD), it pays to defect when the other party's disposition is not known (Hargreaves-Heap, 2004). This is true when the game is not (infinitely) repeated and agents value immediate pay-off higher than their long-term one, that is they have a high future discount factor.

All interactions, or else games, are infinitely repeated or more realistically, and players perceive them as infinitely repeated. When A interacts with B, playing a game such as the PD, and at the same time interacts with C, playing a game such as hawk-dove, his experience from one game is transferred to the other. Therefore, A is a link between the two games or among all the games she plays at any given time and the strategies employed in these games. A's behaviour is affected by the outcome of each interaction and by the behaviour of B, C and so on. If A and B are strangers and they do not expect to meet again, their interaction history will affect their behaviour in their interaction (Leinfellner et al., 1998). Hence, the game they play is affected by the games they had played before they met. Or in other words, the game played between A and B is a sub-game of all the games A and B play and their choices are affected by their history. In this context, A and B never interact in a one-off game, as they perceive every game they play as part of one single large game. All these sub-games are repeated and consequently, mutual cooperation in PD type of games yields the highest pay-off.

A person who does not maximise her utility immediately, does not necessarily behave irrationally. She still behaves rationally provided that based on the knowledge and information she has, she believes her actions will maximise her utility. Her actions or set of strategies are confined by environmental parameters that cannot be influenced by her. Therefore, when evaluating an agent's behaviour, we must take these restrictions into account.

Rationality and maximisation depend primarily on the agent's perception of available strategies and environmental limitations, which in turn depend on available information. Thus, rational agents acting in the same environment should adopt similar strategies. There is no full information in this respect, but there is access to roughly equal information. Each rational agent has access to the same amount of information and therefore should adopt the same strategy in order to maximise her utility. Rational individuals with access to similar information should make similar decisions and adopt similar strategies. This does not assume that preferences have to converge for a convention to be formed; rather it refers to a common understanding of the principles of social interactions. Individuals do not have to have similar preferences and it is likely that they will have conflicting interests. However, equal rationality should lead to a decision-making process that leads to an optimal outcome. Put differently, there is equal rationality within a social group, as opposed to the neoclassical models which assume equal rationality for all.

Furthermore, it is plausible to assert that each agent has roughly the same memory. It does not have to be full memory of every decision in the game's history, but "each individual remembers a general experience of the game but not how he fared against particular opponents" (Sugden, 2004: 60), so that each player has a general understanding of how agents with whom he has interacted behave. And this understanding creates a disposition to act accordingly in the future. If the player has interacted mostly with cooperators (or he believes he has), then it is more likely he will expect his future interactions to be with cooperators.

The most important environmental parameter is other individuals with whom interactions are possible. What is rational depends on the disposition of potential interlocutors; in a group of cooperators it is rational to cooperate, whereas in a group of defectors a rational individual has to defect. Hence, it is important that dispositions are known or accurately predicted.

The longer the history of an interaction, the more likely it is that others' strategies are perceived as known. More realistically each agent participates in a number of interactions. These interactions affect her conception of others' strategies and thus an agent's behaviour. In this context, a rational agent is expected to be able to form an opinion about her environment, and the corresponding maximising strategies.

Not all interactions bear the same weight in rational deliberation. Each interaction has a degree of salience; interactions with many repetitions or high pay-offs are more important than interactions that are short-lived or have low pay-offs respectively. When an agent's interaction collapses after many iterations, she will be more cautious in her new interactions. By doing so, she minimises possible loses from her interactions. Also, when the proportion and gravity of interactions that collapse is high, then a rational agent will be more cautious in her new interactions. For instance, when a short series of interactions collapses, it will not affect old series that have lasted longer. However, the collapse of many interactions, even if they have been short-lived, will have an effect on the agent's perception of her environment and thus her disposition. Repeated interactions within a population highlight the importance of optimal equilibria in relation to individual rationality. To conclude, a rational agent as described above is assumed to have access to roughly the same information as her neighbours, a similar capacity to remember past interactions and evaluate her environment which leads to developing similar maximising strategies for a given environment. Thus, the definition of rational behaviour depends on an agent's environment and maximising strategies are bounded by environmental limitations (Gigerenzer, 2002).

The above discussion of rationality does not necessarily dismiss the premises of strategic interaction between rational utility maximisers. Two interacting individuals behave rationally when the outcome for each one is the best she could have achieved. The Nash equilibrium point is therefore a deterministic outcome if we accept the basic conditions of rationality ceteris paribus. Thus, once we accept that agents are rational and found within the same environment, the outcome of their interaction is known.

In one-shot and finitely repeated PD games, defection is the only Nash equilibrium. However, when the number of iterations is high and information availability is a given, this is not the case. On the contrary, when the number of iterations is finite and known, rational individuals will be able to predict that their opponent will defect at the last round. As a result, both defect in the first round. Therefore, whether it is rational to cooperate depends on the game's specific parameters (Gintis, 2006). We can safely assume that all meaningful interactions occur within a social context. Hence, the condition of interdependence is met. Also, within a social context information spreading is a realistic and plausible assertion, especially in modern interconnected societies. Ultimately, what is rational depends on the social environment where the action takes place.

There are a multitude of parameters that have to be taken into consideration when looking at how social structures come about and how they change. Most of these parameters can be influenced significantly by individual action and even more by the collective action of rational individuals (Elster, 1985). Therefore, it is essential that we use a framework that includes both explanation of collective behaviour, focusing on the behaviour of social groups, and also explanation of the individual behaviour of rational agents.

Contractarian economics

How can morality be defined within economic theory, in a world of self-interested maximisers? Moral behaviour is taken to be a synthesis of ideas introduced by Hume and Hobbes in that it requires rationality and sociability (Gauthier, 1979); social conventions, as the result of repeated interactions between rational agents, serve as a mechanism for information spreading and enforcement, ensuring maximisation within social constraints (Gauthier, 1979). Morality is then not externally imposed, but a pre-condition for maximisation, within the given social boundaries. This stands in opposition to Kantian and to an extent Rawlsian approaches to morality and justice (Morris and Ripstein, 2001). Contractarianism is common in contemporary political philosophy and economic theory; in both cases there is an implicit social contract that regulates behaviour (Kymlicka, 1990). Proponents of the efficiency of free markets accept the idea that mutual advantage is adequate to regulate behaviour in the same way that political and moral contractarians accept that an appeal to reason is sufficient for the establishment of a social contract. As such, contractarianism is unique in its ability to combine rationality and morality. Importantly, contractarianism is unique in its ability to link economic theory and practice with ethical theory. Economic theory is intrinsically contractarian as it relies on the assumption of mutual benefit as a result of interactions between free and rational actors. The tacit agreement in economic theory lies on the fact that all interlocutors are rational and accept the same premises for interaction. Although economics is not generally thought of in contractarian terms, the idea that the two approaches are similar is not new. Pareto optimality is discussed by the so-called Edgeworth box which describes maximisation through the conflict, or else, contract curve. The critical point here is that contractarianism is understood as an implied rather than explicit agreement. Individuals interacting within the same social context share a common understanding of the rules of interaction. For instance, the supply and demand model in economics relies on the assumption that the equilibrium price is reached through the given model. In practice, economic agents operate under the understanding that the price at a supermarket is not negotiable, whereas the price for a used car might be. These unwritten rules of economic behaviour constitute an implied social convention that is in line with the premises of contractarianism.

Although Hobbes's political philosophy relies on individuality and self-interest, Hume's approach is more 'sociable' and 'emotional'. This can create methodological problems when talking about rational agency using Hume. However, Hume's account does invalidate rational agency. For Hume, motives for behaviour do not lie on self-interest but that does not have to lead to the conclusion that behaviour is not maximising. When social conventions facilitate utility maximisation, then behaviour can be seen as rational. Rationality is then linked to outcomes, rather than motives or cognitive processes. Whether a farmer helps his neighbour because he feels it's the 'right' thing to do or because he fears punishment from the Leviathan is not important. What does matter is that he actually helps him and the he maximises when doing so. The conflict between individuality and sociability will be discussed in more detail in Chapters 3 and 4.

Moral contractarianism is a method to derive principles of justice that govern our behaviour, which do not have to agree with specific ideals of justice since they are the outcome of interactions among individuals of similar rationality. A rational agent would not accept a contract if she thought it limits her maximisation. And since all interlocutors would do the same, the final contract will be one that maximises the utility of all contractors given the limitations of social interaction. Therefore, it is a state where social welfare is Pareto efficient. This understanding of justice does not have to be in agreement with any form of cultural understanding of justice. However, the history and culture of a society determines the culture of individuals who draw the contract. Their rationality is defined and limited by their cultural environment. Their ability to deliberate and the availability of information are similar in all members of a group and thus, they are all equally rational.

In Gauthier's *Morals by Agreement* (1986) rationality and justice are presented in terms of a contract, constituting a contractarian theory of rational choice and justice. Contractarianism plays a connecting role; the underlying idea of mutual agreement refers to both rationality and justice. Justice is however broadly understood here as something that agents of roughly equal status would agree on. On the contractarian account any interaction between similarly rational agents is just (Murray, 2007). Thus, contractarianism provides a framework where it is possible to combine justice, as the outcome of moral behaviour, and rationality. In Hobbes's *Leviathan* (1976) the state of nature is used as the starting point and incentive for bargaining. Similarly, in *Morals by Agreement* (1986) bargaining begins at the original position, which is the status-quo to be compared with the eventual share of the cooperative surplus. In the proposed social convention account, the original position will be taken to be the present status-quo which does not need to be idealised or abstract. In economic terms, the equivalent is the existence of a market equilibrium; this equilibrium is seen as the contract, or agreement, point and the absence of a market is the state of nature.

A basic bargaining procedure is defined by the Edgeworth box and Pareto optimality which describe a simplified model of the interaction between two rational individuals. It is valuable because, in its simplicity, it provides a concise description of the possible outcomes of an interaction. There is a single optimal point where both players maximise, but there are many Pareto-efficient points on the aptly named conflict or contract curve connecting all possible outcomes.

Bargaining is central to contractarianism and to the concept of the social contract. Two agents who interact repeatedly will either have to bargain repeatedly over the rules of their interaction or agree that their first agreement will be binding for all their subsequent interactions. However, their interactions will be continuously changing their history and therefore their maximisation strategies. It is more plausible then to assume that agreement points will be more stable when they are decided on a more frequent basis. Each agreement point can be used for a number of interactions. Then a new bargaining procedure can be initiated by either agent when she believes the existing contract is outdated. In this account bargaining is part of the interaction; the agents' repeated bargaining and interactions are part of an enlarged game consisting of periods of negotiation and longer periods of interaction (Binmore, 1998). Assuming repeated interactions implies that interacting agents have similar histories, or at least that each agent's history is known. Therefore their strategy can be predicted. In game theoretical terms, repeated interactions make that the game played cooperative.

Following Binmore's discussion of the Nash bargaining solution – which eventually was accepted by Gauthier as well (Gauthier and Sugden, 1993) – bargaining agents have roughly similar bargaining skills (Binmore, 2007). Their bargaining skills are included in the rationality function and since they act in similar environments their bargaining skill-set will be similar. The bargaining game therefore is symmetric as far as the players' rationality and bargaining powers are concerned. Given repeated interactions, even in the case where bargaining skills are not strictly symmetric, they will converge to being similar enough to not have an impact on their bargaining. Repeated interactions are a trial and error procedure, where the least skilful player has the opportunity to learn and improve. And by reflecting on past interactions, she will be able to improve her bargaining skills. Therefore, once we assume repeated, non-random interactions, bargaining skills are also assumed to be similar. In this respect, bargaining is an evolutionary process, broadly speaking, leading to an equilibrium (Gintis, 2009).

Traditional bargaining premises change once we accept the repetitiveness of interactions. A bargaining problem has a starting point, break-down point and agreement point. Rational agents compare their utilities under each contract point and adopt maximising strategies. In repeated bargaining games, there cannot be a break-down point. In the case where there can be no agreement, agents bargain with someone who is more willing to accept their claims. Rational reflection on the bargaining procedure and the contract point of each interaction results in players choosing whether they will interact with the same person in the future. In this sense, the role of rationality in bargaining is two-fold. Firstly, during bargaining players are assumed to be rational. Secondly, when an agreement point is reached, the contract terms are contrasted with other contracts. Thus, salient maximising strategies will develop. Individuals with similar maximising strategies will tend to bargain with each other giving rise to specific bargaining strategies and solutions. In conclusion, in a repeated interaction framework, bargaining strategies converge and over time rational agents adopt similar strategies. Also, the lines between conventions and contract are blurred in the above analysis; a convention arises through a process similar to a typical contract process and eventually the social contract is theoretically defined similarly to social conventions.

Rational morality

Rationality here is primarily characterised by mutual unconcern; the idea of independence of utility functions or put differently, the idea that one cannot care for one's interlocutors. The starting point is selfish rationality, not Pareto-optimisation (Gauthier, 2013). Economic rationality is qualified so that it fits in the social approach taken. This follows from sociological discussions of rational agency, but here it is done in the context of morality, not just social interactions. Morality, ethics and justice are defined and understood in terms of economic theory and practice, in addition to the importance of social interactions and dynamics. The three concepts are interlinked but separate; moral behaviour leads to just outcomes, whereas ethics describes the socially acceptable norms of behaviour. The common element in all three is the underlying ideas of rational agency, mutual advantage and Pareto efficiency. Economic maximisation is a social activity and as such, must depend on others; in economic theory terms, maximisation is strategic. The idea that all interactions are repeated allows for the introduction of other-regarding motives in rational deliberation and therefore, the inclusion of morality. An implication of the synthesis between rational and moral behaviour is that immorality must be rooted in irrationality, given the social nature of rationality presented here. Moreover, given the approach taken here morality is not to be forced upon people's behaviour and as a result, immoral outcomes are possible. Adam Smith considered human behaviour as the common denominator in ethics and economics. As such, economic behaviour, as described in *The Wealth of Nations*, does not have to separate from other-regarding behaviour that is called for in the *Theory of Material Sentiments*. The argument here is based on similar premises. Agency is independent of whether we are talking about behaviour in the marketplace or the non-economic transaction. Homo-economicus is a rational agent in a market place and homo-sociologicus a social agent in a social setting. However, the same individual can operate in the market and in society at different times; ultimately we talk about different behaviour by the same *individual*, depending on the circumstances. Since it is the same individual, the premises and motivation of her behaviour have the same roots, irrespective of whether she is in the market or a social gathering. These premises are not always self-interested, but when they are they lead to moral outcomes. When they are not self-interested, then it is even more likely that they lead to moral outcomes as the starting point does not have to be one of mutual unconcern (Dimock, 2010).

Rational morality is the basis of the idea that morality can be derived from rationality. The debate on whether this can be true is long dating at least as far back as Plato. Perhaps Adam Smith's work highlights how human behaviour is defined by both moral and rational motives. For Smith, humans can exhibit behaviour that is based on sympathy and self-interest. The following chapters will argue for a rational morality that is the result of social and repeated interactions between self-interested, economic agents aiming at re-establishing economic theory closer to Adam Smith without requiring agents to have moral motives. In this respect, morality is a side-effect of rationality and the motives of one's behaviour are not necessarily in moral accordance to the outcomes (Schelling, 2006).

3 Moral economics
Constrained maximisation

Rational constraints on maximising behaviour can be shown to lead to moral outcomes. There are two differences with most of the literature on the ethics of economics. First, the constraints are rational, not moral or value based. Second, the constraints are internal, not externally imposed. Constrained maximisation as a method to ground moral behaviour on rationality was introduced by David Gauthier in *Morals by Agreement* (1986).

The origin of normativity

Normative rules must be rooted in self-interest to be binding. The alternative would be arbitrary and authoritative. Adam Smith (Smith and Haakonssen, 2002) and more recently John Rawls (Rawls, 2005) appealed to the idea of an 'ideal observer' to justify normative rules. Their argument lies on the idea that if there could be an observer unaffected by social constraints and prejudices, her moral prescriptions would be binding for all of us; the mere fact that she is found outside society makes her normative judgement significant.

However, normative rules derived from within a society are more powerful than rules that rely on asocial or pre-social premises. David Gauthier's moral contractarianism is based on similar premises that rely on individual rationality (Vallentyne, 1991); a contract or agreement between rational, utility maximisers holds more strength than any alternative. Rational agents who have agreed to follow a set of moral rules within a society have a rational imperative to actually follow these rules (Nida-Rümelin and Spohn, 2000). Thus, the proposed account of a social morality is reinforced and supported by self-interest. As long as agents are rational, they have reasons to be moral. Social normativity is further enhanced by incorporating the concepts of repeated interactions, a plausible and pragmatic parameter of social interactions (Katz, 2000). Rational agents are seen to interact in repeated, non-random interaction, similar to interactions that take place in actual social groups – this concept will be further explored in Chapter 3 on sociability. The moral contractarian paradigm that relies on rational individuals accepting and following moral rules is put in a social context when we consider interacting agents operating in a social environment.

The repetitiveness of social interactions leads to the validity and acceptance of the norms regulating them. When these norms prove ineffective, the respective social interactions collapse and a new set of interactions can lead to new norms. Hume's story of two farmers helping each other better illustrates this idea (Hume, 1985). If each farmer helps the other, then over time and perhaps over generations, cooperative rules become the social norm. If the established norm is no longer followed for whatever reason, interactions between farmers may lead to a different social norm. The implication of this approach is that moral rules depend on social interactions and as a result they are relative to the given social context. So, moral rules and norms are society-specific and are only binding within the specific society or social group. Hume's account does not contradict the assumption of rational agency. The farmers behave rationally in that they maximise their utility by following the established norm – for however long they think that is the case.

There can be no ideal observer or reasonable agreement that relies on asocial premises determining normative principles, without a violation of individual agency and reason. Interlocutors build the framework for society's moral norms through repeated interactions and the resulting social structures. Moral rules that are not the pragmatic, actual outcome of these social interactions are not truly binding as they rely on asocial principles to enforce social behaviour. On the contrary, moral norms that are the result of repeated interactions among utility maximisers are binding as long as individuals remain self-interested. Hence, there can be no universally objective normative principles but only society-specific objective moral norms, which may in time become universal through their expansion (Skyrms, 2004).

Adam Smith and John Harsanyi before John Rawls argued in a similar way about the existence of an objective way to assess the morality of an action. Perhaps Smith and Harsanyi were closer to the account proposed here in that they argued for an observer bound by social circumstances as opposed to Rawls's ideal observer. The present argument goes further calling for a social observer, who is furthermore rational just like all other individuals in society. Empathy is in this respect an obstacle for morality as Bloom (2018) argues. Rationality is the only basis for social interaction and morality that can be objective and thus binding.

The proposed account is a bottom-up approach as it starts from interactions between individuals which gradually may become accepted first on a group level and then on a broader, society level. As such, it is in contrast to centralised, Kantian/Rawlsian approaches that prescribe a single normative truth, which comes from divine providence or a single line of reasoned argumentation. An approach to moral norms that is based on the individualistic account of Hobbes (Hobbes, 1976) in conjunction with the Humean approach to social conventions relies exclusively on individual rationality and social interactions. Morality is, in this respect, a social equilibrium as determined by repeated social interactions among rational, utility maximisers.

There can be no universal moral norms dictated by reason or theoretical arguments coming from above or based on asocial premises. If there can be a universal morality this has to be built from the ground up; topical moral norms that develop and take over can lead to a universal morality that is powerful, compelling and applicable in a social context.

Constrained maximisation

Constrained maximisation yields optimal outcomes while maximising individual utility within a given environment. Constraining one's maximisation is rational given that others also constrain their maximisation. An interaction between constrained maximisers yields higher utility for the individuals by comparison to straightforward maximisation, while at the same time leading to a socially optimal outcome. Hobbes's Leviathan forces individuals to keep their agreements. On the contrary, Gauthier speaks of voluntary rational compliance; the contractors should keep their agreement because rationality dictates it without the need for external enforcement. Gauthier's argument on compliance is based on the idea of constrained maximisation.

A constrained maximiser will choose a strategy that does not strictly maximise her utility if she knows others behave similarly. This enables her to participate in future interactions with constrained maximisers, thus increasing her overall benefit (Gauthier, 1986.). In other words, constrained maximisation is a strategy of conditional cooperation. In addition, constrained maximisation is rational behaviour. A constrained maximiser is still rational but "reasons in a different way" (Gauthier: 170). Moreover, a constrained maximiser will only accept a small decrease in her immediate utility, aiming at long-term gains from interactions (Hartogh, 1993). Constrained maximisers as opposed to straightforward ones comply with an agreement that requires them not to maximise their utility, provided they think that the other members in the contract will adopt the same strategy. Therefore, constrained maximisation rests on the assumption that rational agents adopt joint strategies in order to maximise. The rational behaviour of one individual depends on the strategy employed by the other.

In terms of a prisoner's dilemma game, constrained maximisation is cooperative behaviour. Cooperation in repeated Prisoner's Dilemma (PD) games is maximising, provided that both players cooperate. Cooperators are more likely to be accepted in an agreement, as all parties in the agreement will prefer to interact with agents who are disposed to cooperate. Since cooperation leads to optimal equilibria, it is rational for all parties to be disposed to enter a cooperative agreement. Therefore, a constrained maximising strategy gives the advantage of being accepted in a cooperative agreement and hence optimising joint strategies. Provided the agents are fully informed, constrained maximisation yields a greater utility over a series of interactions. Interactions between constraint maximisers lead to higher *cooperative surplus* making it socially rational to cooperate.

Constrained maximisation only works when constrained maximisers are able to identify others who are similarly disposed. The presupposition that the agents' disposition to cooperate or defect is known poses problems to the plausibility of the argument that constrained maximisation is rational. In a more realistic setting, dispositions can only be known at a probability in a society which includes both constrained and straightforward maximisers. In this case, there can be four possible outcomes from bargaining: non-cooperation, cooperation, defection and exploitation. The ability to be fully informed becomes critical. If cooperators can identify each other, then they will commit to agreement among themselves. In this case, straightforward maximisers will not be able to maximise their utility through entering agreements. Once more, the existence of a social environment that facilitates repetitiveness of interactions as well as information spreading is critical. In conclusion, constrained maximisation is a rational strategy when others are similarly disposed to constrain their maximisation, given disposition translucency. Constrained maximisation is a moral constraint that is grounded on rational premises. However, it is made clear that this does not include all moral behaviour or moral institutions. Constrained maximisation is not always rational. Constrained maximisers have to recognise and decline interactions with straightforward maximisers in order to achieve utility maximisation. Constrained maximisation, however, does not require rational agent to prioritise anything but their self-interest. As such, the qualification on rational agency by comparison to standard economic theory is minor. The implications of constrained maximisation, sociability and time dynamics are perhaps more ambitious departures from mainstream economics. These will be discussed in more detail in Chapters 3 and 4.

Constrained maximisation is criticised both for being a moral, not rational, constraint and for not being strong enough to enforce moral behaviour on self-regarding utility maximisers. Constrained maximisation reduces a moral rule of behaviour to a rational one and is seen as a "core element in the agent's overarching life plan" (Gauthier in Gauthier and Sugden 1993: 188), but this contradicts rational agency as accepted by economists, which requires immediate maximisation. Moreover, instrumental rationality is at odds with the principle of constrained maximisation (Hollis, 1994). In the economic account of rationality, rational behaviour leads to utility maximisation. On the contrary, constrained maximisation is rational because it promotes utility. Once a constrained maximiser finds herself in an agreement with a similarly disposed agent, it is rational for her to turn into a straightforward maximiser. The only way to avoid this gap is to use expressive instead of instrumental rationality (Verbeek, 2002). An agent who is disposed to cooperate does not have to cooperate all the way through a series of interactions; he may defect from the agreement once he benefits from others' constrained maximising behaviour. Practical rationality cannot provide a bargaining solution as disposition to behave morally depends on how one expects others to behave. However, wishing that others cooperate does not make any difference. Thus, it is unlikely that rational dispositions will lead to moral behaviour (Nida-Rumelin, in Gauthier and Sugden, 1993). As such, rational compliance is as problematic in that it is not in accordance with the assumptions of practical rationality and rational agency as these are perceived by traditional economic theory (Kavka, 1983).

Similarly, Hampton (1988) exposes the problem of compliance in the contractarian approach: the difficulty in keeping one's promises without an external enforcer. She argues that it is not important whether individuals behave based on rationality or passions since the outcome in both cases will be defection from the agreement. If humans are motivated by passions such as fear, they have no reason to behave differently after the contract. In this case, they will not comply with the agreement, even if they have agreed to it. In the case where individuals are rational actors living in a non-cooperative state of nature, there is no incentive for them to cooperate after they have benefited from a contract.

So, constrained maximisation does not come without any issues. However, it is an improvement on economic understanding of economic rationality because it allows for rational agents to consider their social environment and the dynamics of time, through joint strategy. In doing so, constrained maximisation allows to combine homo economicus with versions of homo sociologicus. Also, it is an improvement on accounts of rational morality and morality more broadly as it is based on self-interest and selfish individuals to build an account of morality that does not require agents to have a moral predisposition.

The rationality of constrained maximisation

Constrained maximisation as introduced in *Morals by Agreement* (1986) is problematic because it assumes dispositional translucency and it does not adequately justify the move from economic rationality to constrained maximisation. A conventionalist approach that requires agents to know others past behaviour can replace the need for disposition translucency and therefore justify constrained maximisation from a purely rational standpoint. Sugden's account of convention as a "stable equilibrium in a game that has two or more stable equilibria" (Sugden 2004: 32) recognises the importance of social dynamics and repeated interactions and, just like the argument for constrained maximisation, is based on a game theoretical analysis. Thus, it is more appropriate to use in the present context.

Rational agents are expected to constrain their maximisation in order to benefit from cooperative ventures for mutual advantage. Thus, rational maximisers become constrained maximisers. A constrained maximiser is "conditionally disposed to cooperate in ways that, followed by all, would yield nearly optimal and fair outcomes, and does cooperate in such ways when she may actually expect to benefit" (Gauthier, 1986: 177). Instead of maximising her utility immediately, a constrained maximiser chooses to participate in cooperative ventures and therefore transfer her maximisation into the future. Given that the overall pay-off for a constrained maximiser is higher than the present pay-off for a straightforward maximiser, constrained maximisation is still justifiable from a rational choice theory perspective. And in this sense constrained maximisation does not have to be considered a non-rational principle or a moral constraint. "The constrained maximiser … reasons in a different way" (Gauthier, 1986: 170), but still reasons in accordance with the demands of rationality. It is, however, a weak principle from a rational choice perspective: the traditional rational choice paradigm expects agents to maximise their utility in every interaction.

Constrained maximisation is based on agents' dispositions being translucent. Translucency is more realistic than transparency under "realistically possible" conditions; "persons are neither transparent nor opaque" (Gauthier, 1986: 174) and as a result they can guess others' disposition at a high probability. Moreover, it is explicitly stated that "[w]e want to relate our idealizing assumptions to the real world" (Gauthier, 1986: 174). Therefore, for Gauthier assuming translucency is preferable to assuming transparency. However, there is no argument justifying the plausibility of dispositional translucency or explaining how this skill comes about. The mere fact that translucency is more plausible than transparency does not necessarily make it plausible enough. If dispositions are not translucent or otherwise perceptible by other agents, then the central argument for the rationality of CM fails.

The account of CM presented in *Morals by Agreement* is problematic on two accounts. First, because it relies on the possibility of disposition translucency, which is implausible and impossible to relate to real world circumstances. A rational individual will choose to constrain her maximisation, only when she knows others will do the same. Even if we accept this can be achieved in some interactions, it is impossible for the majority of our interactions. Subsequently, disposition translucency is essential for agents to become constrained maximisers. If dispositions are not translucent to begin with, a rational agent has no reason to be a constrained maximiser. Second, CM is problematic in that its instrumental rationality credentials are weak; constrained maximisers reason differently but their "enlightenment" is not justified or explained. In that sense a constrained maximiser is a moral agent as her deliberation includes others utility.

The conventionalist account presented here offers a stronger argument for CM. A constrained maximiser is only interested in furthering her interests with no other consideration. Rational agents choose with whom they will interact, based on past interactions and not on predicting others' strategies. The argument that constrained maximisation can be reconciled with a theory of social conventions requires an analysis of individual rationality in a conventionalist context. And it is to the first of these that I now turn.

Maximisation and rationality are linked to the concept of repeated interactions. Constrained maximisers, by participating in cooperative ventures with other similarly disposed agents, obtain benefits that are not available to straightforward maximisers. Moreover, in terms of maximisation they maximise through participating in cooperative ventures. Hence, embedded in the concept of CM is the idea of a small future discount factor. Constrained maximisers have a future small discount factor in order to prefer future to present maximisation. Although not explicitly presented as such by Gauthier, constrained maximisers are future orientated; they are willing to forfeit the immediate benefit of straightforward maximisation to participate in "cooperative ventures for mutual advantage" (Gauthier, 1986: 179), which are implied to take place in the future. Constrained maximisers exhibit a behaviour that is very similar to prudence despite its rationale being more nuanced than that.

Small future discount factor together with 'joint strategy', another key component of CM, can be best understood in the context of repeated games. Rational agents adopt strategies depending on the strategies of the agents with whom they interact. A rational agent will cooperate with someone who is also disposed to cooperate in order to share a cooperative surplus; "to agree to cooperate is to agree to employ a joint strategy rather than an individual strategy" (Gauthier, 1986: 166). The dividend of this surplus has to be greater in the long run than the outcome of straightforward maximisation. When two agents expect to interact again in the future, cooperation becomes more likely and future maximisation is a rational choice.

A person who does not maximise her utility at a given moment, does not necessarily behave irrationally. She still behaves rationally provided that, based on the knowledge and information she has, she believes her actions will maximise her utility over time. Her actions or set of strategies are limited by environmental parameters that cannot be changed by her. Therefore, when evaluating her behaviour, we must take these restrictions into account. But even then the predictability of her behaviour cannot be a given. The amount of information she possesses and the perception of the strategy restrictions in place, make accurate prediction extremely difficult. Thus we cannot discuss predicting a rational agent's behaviour as if it were a natural science experiment. Prediction is of course possible; and when we know the history of an agent's interactions, successful prediction becomes even more likely. However, we have to bear in mind that rationality and maximisation depend on the agent's perception of the available strategies and environmental limitations. What we can say is that we expect rational agents acting in the same environment to make the same decisions. There is no full information in this respect, but there is equal information. Each rational agent has access to the same amount of information and therefore should adopt the same strategy in order to maximise her utility. Furthermore, each agent can remember roughly the same number of past interactions; if one can remember most of her past interactions, then there is no reason to assume that other agents have a significantly longer or shorter memory; "each individual remembers a general experience of the game but not how he fared against particular opponents" (Sugden, 2004: 60). In other words, each player has a general understanding of how agents with whom he has interacted have behaved. And this understanding creates a disposition to act accordingly in the future. If an agent has (or believes he has) interacted mostly with cooperators, then it is more likely he will expect his future interactions to be with cooperators.

Constrained maximisation as convention

In the conventionalist account of rationality, the reasons behind constrained maximisation are not important. Behaviour is evaluated over time. In this sense there can be no misconception of one's dispositions. A non-cooperator in the first instance has the prospect to change into a cooperator and vice-versa. Whether the change occurred as a response to others' behaviour or not, is irrelevant. What matters is the action itself and more importantly one's behaviour in a series of interactions. In the context of repeated interactions what is important is an agent's strategy over a series of interactions. A non-cooperator in one interaction is not necessarily perceived as non-cooperator in a series of interactions, if she mostly cooperates. In a number of simultaneous interactions, one can cooperate in some and not cooperate in others. The perceived behaviour of an agent will depend on the salience, frequency and longevity of each series of cooperative or non-cooperative interactions.

The most important environmental parameter is other individuals with whom interactions are possible. Therefore, maximising behaviour depends on what the other players are expected to do. When the other players' strategies are not known or are only known at a probability, rational behaviour is not as straightforward a process. The longer the history of an interaction, the more likely it is that the other agents' strategies will be perceived as known. Again, however, in a more realistic setting, we will have to take into account that each agent participates in a number of interactions with different agents. These interactions affect her conception of others' strategies and thus her behaviour. Each interaction has a degree of salience that depends on the duration and the changes it makes to the agent's utility. An agent with a history of many cooperative interactions is more likely to follow cooperative strategies in the future. This is in essence a rewording of Gauthier's argument; CM is rational when there are enough constrained maximisers with whom an agent who is disposed to constrain his maximisation can interact. A history of CM is likely to lead to an equilibrium of CM.

Interacting individuals behave rationally when the outcome for each one is the best they could have achieved. If they know each others' dispositions then maximisation is more likely. A Nash equilibrium point is reached when all agents adopted their maximising strategy; therefore it can be said to be deterministic. Once we accept that the interacting agents are rational actors within the same environment, the outcome of their interaction can be known. There cannot be a rational incentive to move from a Nash equilibrium. In one-shot and finitely repeated prisoner's dilemma games, defection is the only Nash equilibrium. However, when the number of iterations is high and the future discount factor low, the sum of the outcomes of cooperative rounds can exceed the loss occurred at the last round. The benefit of cooperation times the number of iterations can be greater than the cost from cooperating with a defector once. And this is more likely in a population of pairwise interactions and full information. However, when the number of iterations is known, rational individuals will be able to predict that their opponent will defect at the last round. The Nash equilibrium in PD type games of known finite interactions is defection. As a result, both will defect at the first round. It becomes clear therefore, that whether it is rational to cooperate depends on the specific game's parameters. If the benefits of cooperation and the number of iterations are high, then it is very likely that cooperation is rational.

In every interaction there is a cost of rational deliberation; agents have to calculate their benefit from either cooperating or defecting and try to predict others' strategies. The decisions we have to make are not so often about eating a pear or an apple. Rather we have to decide whether planting an apple tree or a pear tree will be more profitable in the long run. A farmer who has to make a rational decision about whether he should invest on apples or pears will have to take into account a large amount of information relating to the economy and the environment. It is of course impossible to have all the information required, but it is completely rational for one to try to gather as much information as possible before making a decision. This is costly and time consuming. It is rational to use others' experiences if the information costs are too high. If apple growers make a bigger profit, then it is rational for a farmer to grow apple trees even without taking into account specific and specialised evidence. The salience of a decision and the level of uncertainty about future conditions may make it worthwhile to undertake the information cost. In this context, it is rational to do what others do and plant apple trees when information is very expensive and the future very uncertain. In short, it is rational to follow the established norms of behaviour rather than deliberate afresh about every single decision.

Individuals act in groups or societies where it is expected to follow conventions of behaviour. Non-conventional behaviour is irrational for two reasons: first, there is punishment that makes non-conventional behaviour costly. Second, stable conventions are the result of interaction among rational individuals. Thus, they are a method of maximising individual and not just group utility. Therefore, it is necessary to discuss how rationality can be understood in the context of conventional behaviour.

The visibility of one's disposition is not, in the conventionalist account, as much of a problem as it is in Gauthier's theory or for mainstream accounts of rational agency for that matter. Within a convention that defines the boundaries of behaviour everyone maximises by acting conventionally. Put differently, everyone behaves as if everybody else will behave conventionally. Thus, agents act conventionally and also rationally when deliberating over defection. Therefore, dispositions become a secondary issue, despite this account being very close conceptually to the rationality of CM in a group of constrained maximisers.

Looking at the stag hunt game can reinforce the argument. If the pay-off of hunting hare is 3 and the pay-off of cooperatively hunting stag is 4, everybody would hunt stag when they expect everybody else to do the same. This brings us back to the problem of disposition translucency. Assuming that a stag hunt was possible during the first interaction, those who decided to hunt hare will not be accepted in the stag hunt, in the next hunt. After repeated hunts the individual pay-off from hunting stag will be greater than the pay-off from hunting hare. This results in stag hunting becoming the dominant strategy. If stag hunting were impossible at the beginning, this society would reach a hare hunting equilibrium. It is up to individual rationality of its members then, to imitate a more successful society that has established a stag hunt. Similarly, in a repeated prisoner's dilemma, if one defects the first time the game is played, then it should be expected that the second time both will defect and the game will result in a non-cooperative equilibrium. If a cooperative equilibrium had been established instead both would be maximising their utility in a repeated game.

In discussing CM, Gauthier says: "The just person [...] has internalized the idea of mutual benefit" (Gauthier, 1986: 157). CM is therefore based on the idea that rational agents have made fairness part of their rational deliberation. And fairness is not distinguished, at least in this account, from morality. In other words, Gauthier stipulates that rational agents have made morality part of their decision making process when they interact with similarly disposed agents. A similar but more plausible assertion can be made for the rational and just person in a socially dynamic context. The just person conforms to conventional rules, because, being rational, she wants to avoid deliberation costs and conventional punishment. Repeated interactions within a small population ensure free riders are found and excluded, and thus knowing each other's dispositions is not a central condition of "constrained maximisation". Within this given group, conventional behaviour is a given. Interactions evolve as individuals grow, learn and gain experience. This has an impact on the way individuals interact. Repeated interactions create dynamics that have an effect on the possible strategies and outcomes of a game, such as trust and social bonds. Gauthier argues that an action is rational when the final outcome of a series of interactions is maximising, irrespective of the outcome of each single action. Sociability and intertemporality also move the centre of interest from the specific action to the final outcome of the interactions that lead to a social equilibrium.

In the conventionalist account, disposition visibility is not essential. The fact that cooperators or non-cooperators form groups that follow conventions makes it highly unlikely that these conventions will be broken. What is more important, breaking these conventions of behaviour is very costly. Rational reflective individuals can see how breaking an equilibrium will only pay in the short term. Within their group they will be punished by being excluded from future conventions. A population will only abandon the status-quo for a Pareto superior equilibrium point. Therefore, the behaviour inside this population can only change through imitation of a more successful interaction structure. An individual learns which strategies are maximising through a trial and error process of repeated interactions. She does not have to know others' incentives or utilities functions. If agent A performs an action X every time agent B performs Y, then B will learn to expect X from A when she performs Y. Agent B only needs to know whether performing Y is maximising and not why A performs X.

Rationality as understood by Gauthier – when he discusses constrained and straightforward maximisation in relevance with the disposition of the population as a whole – is very close to the understanding of social rationality. Gauthier implicitly takes a holistic perspective when defending CM: "A straightforward maximiser [...] must expect to be excluded from co-operative arrangements..." (Gauthier, 1986: 187). Individual rationality is seen in relation to other agents' behaviour. Whether it is rational for one to be a constrained or straightforward maximiser depends exclusively on the behaviour of others; thus, the point of analysis is a pair or a group of interacting agents, not just the individual. It is rational and constrains maximisation in a population of constrained maximisers. And it is also rational to be a straightforward maximiser in a population of straightforward maximisers. Rationality thus depends on the strategies employed by the whole population and not on just one individual.

A society, having adopted a convention, maximises social welfare given historical limitations. Within this society individuals behave conventionally. However, since this account has not abandoned the individual capability for rational deliberation, we have to address the issue of free-riding in large groups such as modern societies. Detection and subsequent punishment in these conditions is difficult and at times unlikely. So it pays for one not to participate in the creation of the co-operative surplus but to be a recipient of its distribution. However, even in large groups the majority of interactions take place among a rather small circle of individuals. Repeated interactions among individuals who know each other and each other's strategies ensure conventional behaviour. When an individual interacts with agents outside the group of frequently encountered agents, her behavioural history is or can be known. If she decides to free-ride in these interactions, she can expect to be excluded from interactions within her 'circle'. Rational agents maximise through the existence of conventions and, therefore, it is rational to uphold those conventions. When my neighbour helps me with my corn and I help him with his, he has a rational incentive to stop interacting with me, if he learns that I cheat in my tax return. Although my cheating does not affect him immediately, he will choose to interact with someone who abides to the same rules as him. And by doing so, he punishes me. This account excludes agents who behave like parasites; constantly moving from one convention to the other, maximising their utility by hiding their true intentions. In this case Gauthier's translucency is more efficient. However, parasitic behaviour is costly because it requires constant movement. Moreover, intra-conventional communication can make the detection of parasites more plausible.

All interactions are related through the agents that participate in them. Therefore, my free-riding in one game will have an effect on another game in which I participate. In the case that my neighbour decides that it is in her best interest also to cheat in her tax return, then our interaction remains intact. This can lead to a new social equilibrium where nobody pays taxes. If this state is preferred to the previous one then it will be the new equilibrium. If not, then rational agents will establish new conventions of behaviour. The processes are not always linear. The status-quo can move to Pareto inferior or superior equilibrium points. However, rational agents are able learn and imitate more successful conventions. A society at a Pareto sub-optimum equilibrium will imitate one at a Pareto optimum equilibrium. Rational agents will follow strategies that maximise individual utility and social welfare, provided they have adequate information. A Pareto superior equilibrium as a result of constrained maximisation will then be imitated by populations of rational agents.

Rationality in the context of social conventions can replace rationality as constrained maximisation. Rationality does not necessarily collide with holistic explanations of behaviour. A rational agent can preserve her rationality and maximise social welfare while maximising individual utility. Her ability to reflect on past actions, of both herself and the agents with whom she interacts, makes it possible to select future strategies and groups. Knowing others' past behaviour is a more realistic assertion than being able to predict their disposition. If we accept this, we can see how rational agents will choose to interact with those of similar history. And this leads to the establishment of equilibria that define a set of available strategies. These social conventions evolve themselves. The more efficient ones are imitated and replicated.

This is not necessarily an optimistic account of human interactions. Depending on the original circumstances, a society can be led to a cooperative or non-cooperative stable equilibrium. It is then up to the rationality of, and the information available to, individual agents to select new strategies or interact with or in new groups. And when an adequate number of agents do so, then the convention evolves. This analysis provides a solution to the problems of constrained maximisation, namely disposition translucency and the need for an adequate number of constrained maximisers. Persons are still expected to constrain their maximisation, but not because they can guess others' dispositions, but because they can know others' past behaviour.

4 Sociability

For Adam Smith, individuals operate within a society and therefore, they are influenced by others and by social norms. However, mainstream economic theory does not examine the impact of society on individual behaviour. Therefore, looking at how social structures affect individual behaviour and rational maximisation will provide a link between the origins of economic theory and its contemporary understanding. In addition, examining individual behaviour in the framework of sociability will offer an essential stepping stone for the argument that morality is the result of rationality and interactions between rational individuals.

The current chapter examines collective action, collective intentionality and the impact of social structures on individual rational choice. The argument is that an action that is deemed rational for an isolated Robinson Crusoe is not necessarily also rational for an economic agent who operates within a society. All interactions are assumed to take place in a social context and as such, are iterated. As a result, interactions represented by the Prisoner's Dilemma (PD) game are maximising when they are cooperative. In Binmore's aphorism the PD is solved if we turn it into a different game (Binmore in Gauthier and Sugden, 1993). The argument here is that in interactions that take place within social groups, the PD is not an accurate representation of human behaviour, nor does it allow us to accurately predict and examine it. An adjusted version of the game that considers the impact of sociability is more appropriate and can offer more useful insights. Sociability proves to be the link between moral and rational behaviour, in the vein of Adam Smith's work but more explicitly and using a game theoretical framework to examine interactions.

In this understanding, cooperation in the PD game is very close to morality. However, there is one fundamental difference; cooperation refers to interlocutors in one or a series of interactions. Morality on the other hand, refers to internalising and expressing cooperative behaviour throughout one's interactions within society and punishing defectors. Given repeated interactions within a given social structure, one cooperates by default and without expecting cooperative behaviour in return by the given interlocutor. Whereas cooperation is a strategy that can be adopted reciprocally, morality is a type of behaviour that is adopted throughout one's life interactions.

In the proposed understanding, moral behaviour is not exclusively cooperation in a PD game. Moral behaviour is dictated and defined by the established social equilibrium; given repeated interactions and information availability the efficient social equilibrium, which ensures individual utility maximisation, must be a cooperative one.

The fact that the argument for rational morality relies on free individuals interacting within the bounds of social structures, an established social equilibrium that is Pareto efficient but not optimal, must be accepted as moral. The opposite would require pre-existing notions of morality thus violating the idea that rational individuals reach mutually beneficial outcomes. Given time and information, we should expect that social equilibria are Pareto optimal, but rational morality can only ensure efficiency. As such, we will have to agree that an established social status that is accepted by free individuals meets rational morality criteria. As with the case of cooperation and morality, the outcome of rational agents interacting over time must be Pareto optimal and thus, moral.

Social morality

Singer's drowning child example can describe how sociability is understood. In the typical example, it all about the responsibility and the behaviour of the passer-by to either save or ignore the child. In the current context, it is assumed that this is an interaction between two responsible agents. That does not have to lead to different results in the moral evaluation of the situation but the original example seems to imply that the child is not an agent and as such, the passer-by is the only morally responsible agent in the situation. The implication of sociability is that all interactions whose scope is discussed here, must have at least two moral agents. Moreover, the ethical scope of the example changes when we consider that this is a repeated interaction; if the same agents have to save the same child every day, then the moral argument for saving the child is not straightforward – although one might still find it difficult to argue that it is moral to ignore the child. In a slightly more pragmatic setting and in the context of the current argument for sociability and rationality, we can imagine a situation where children ignore warning to avoid risky waters and as a result they need to be saved by passers-by. Now this changes the original example in two ways; first, it turns it into a repeated interaction and second, it is about random individuals from a social group and not two specific agents. Again, the argument for what constitutes moral behaviour is similar, although weakened. The passer-by is still morally obliged to save the child; however, there seems to be a moral obligation by the child's parents to take pre-emptive measures. More to the point, it is easy to argue that there is responsibility on social scale to take measures that inhibit children from approaching the water.

The above assumes that within the given society information is readily available. Everybody knows that children risk their lives by approaching the water. So, there are two questions arising. Is there a moral responsibility for a rational agent to save a child drowning, given that this is either a repeated occurrence or that the child actively tried to bypass and measures in place to block access to the water?

Spontaneous order

Spontaneous order, a phrase first used by Hayek (Sugden, 2004), describes very adequately the main aim of *The Economics of Rights, Cooperation and Welfare* (Sugden, 2004): to show that social interactions can lead to equilibria of moral behaviour without third party enforcement. The core of the argument is that societies, just like ideal markets, reach efficient and optimal equilibria should they be left to operate freely. In this framework, a convention is a "stable equilibrium in a game that has two or more stable equilibria" (Sugden, 2004: 32).

Society reaches an equilibrium when all its members, or almost all of them, follow their maximising strategy. The majority of a population has to adopt the conventional behaviour in order for the convention to become established. The greater the number of individuals that follow a convention the more likely it is that this convention will expand, until it becomes a social convention that is generally followed. The implication here is that conventions arise and become stable randomly and not so much because of individual rational deliberation. What matters is the establishment of a convention so as to regulate social interactions and avoid conflict and not the selection of a specific convention. In conclusion, the type of convention and the equilibrium point are not important. What matters in this analysis is their becoming established and stable. There are different types of conventions with various structures and equilibrium points.

Sugden distinguishes three categories of conventions: conventions of coordination, conventions of property and conventions of reciprocity (Sugden, 2004). They are all seen as equilibria of repeated games whose purpose is social peace by generating an understanding of justice. The break of conventional behaviour is viewed as unjust by those who follow it, as it is the convention in the first place that has created a sense of what is just. The breaking of a convention for whatever reason, either by mistake or weaknesses of will or because it is deemed irrational, creates a feeling of injustice to others, as established conventions serve as social behaviour regulators. Since it is rational to keep conventions as long as others keep them, it follows that is also rational for one to want others to keep the convention (ibid).

Conventions are characterised as moral and rational: "...conventions are normally maintained by both interest and morality..." (Sugden, 2004: 155). They come about as the result of rational interaction, but rationality alone cannot sustain them. In a sense, in Sugden's work our sense of morality is being informed by established conventions, which are also the outcome of rational interactions. Moreover, since there is no equilibrium selection mechanism provided, an established convention while maximising for its members may very well be random, not moral. In other words, rationality leads to conventions of justice through an arbitrary evolutionary path. In this respect, Sugden's approach is close to constrained maximisation. They both justify a constrained rational behaviour that is not always maximising, based on interactions with other rational agents who are disposed to behave in the same way in *Morals by Agreement*, or have been behaving in the same way in *The Economics of Rights, Cooperation and Welfare* (Sugden, 2004). Sugden uses game theory more formally and extensively than Gauthier. This has an impact on his use of the idea of morality which is evidently more difficult to incorporate in formal analysis (Braithwaite, 1955). Justice for Sugden is a side effect of the interactions between rational agents. Thus, moral behaviour is the outcome of rationality and does serve as its constraint. Morality is the result of spontaneous order that arises in the form of natural, and not designed, conventions. Sugden manages to show that it is plausible to assert that social order does not depend on an external enforcer and that conventions of justice are self-enforced once they become established.

The stag hunt

Although *The Stag Hunt and the Evolution of the Social Structure* (Skyrms, 2004) is not directly linked to moral behaviour or contractarianism, it can be used to link rational morality to social behaviour and the interdependence between the two. As we have seen, constrained maximisation is rational provided interactions occur between similarly disposed agents. In other words it is rational for one to be disposed to behave as a constrained maximiser if one is in a group of constrained maximisers. Skyrms's analysis describes a similar concept of equilibria that depend on the behaviour of a critical mass of agents and utility maximisation as a function of his neighbours' strategies.

In *The Stag Hunt and the Evolution of the Social Contract* (ibid) concepts such as morality and justice are not discussed directly. Instead, the focus is on cooperation and cooperative equilibria. Skyrms's main aim is not to show how morality can arise from rational premises but to argue that social cooperative equilibria incorporate individual maximisation. Morality and especially rational morality as presented in the first chapter is closely related with cooperation as introduced by Skyrms. For Skyrms rationality "is not necessary for solving the social contract" (Skyrms, 2004: xii), but cooperative equilibria are the result of correlated dynamics between social structures and individual strategies. Despite the similar aims, Skyrms adopts naturalistic premises about individual rationality, social interactions and the social contract.

Skyrms, just like Aristotle and Hobbes before him, accepts that animal societies have solved the problem of peaceful coexistence by adhering to natural social contracts, that is, social contracts that are defined and bound by the natural characteristics of each species. On the contrary, human social contracts are artificial and in conflict with human nature since humans are naturally self-interested and outside family and social circles mutually unconcerned. The idea that humans are naturally self-interested might be contentious for some. I do not wish to make any sweeping claims about human nature and human behaviour; the argument here relies on assuming that humans are selfish; the morality of the outcome of interactions among selfish individuals is not threatened by the existence of altruistic agents. Assuming the worse, or in this case self-interest, about human behaviour is only meant to serve as the baseline rather than incorporate all human behaviour. If all people are selfish and the result of their interactions is moral, then the same will apply when not all people are selfish and even when none is selfish.

Rational, self-interested agents realise that their self-interest is at odds with collective benefit and as Hobbes (1976) argued, human social contracts fail because of rationality (Hardin, 1968). In this respect, rationality threatens the stability of the social equilibrium, which is sustained by the dynamics of social structures. In addition, the prisoner's dilemma game, which is commonly used to describe social interactions, is not as effective in describing dynamic interactions within social groups as the stag hunt game. The former describes two person interactions whereas the latter examines interactions at a social scale. The stag hunt, originally an allegory used by Rousseau, is "a prototype of the social contract" (Skyrms, 2004: 1). A tribe has to decide whether they should hunt stag or hare. Stag hunting requires everybody to participate and is therefore a joint decision. If the tribe decides to hunt stag collectively, they will need all the available hunters to participate, but collective action is not necessary for hare hunting; on the contrary hare hunting implies collective action failure. Unlike the typical PD analysis, the stag hunt discusses a group of people thus making it easier to examine issues regarding collective and individual maximisation.

The stag hunt example shows how individual rationality contradicts social welfare and is more directly linked to the problem of free-riding. The cooperative social contract is sustained if the tribe collectively hunts for stags. A stag hunt equilibrium can be destabilised by a large enough number of hare hunters. The critical number of stag hunters needed depends on the formal representation of the game. However, the implication is that in order for a cooperative social structure to be sustained, it is essential that a majority agrees and behaves according to the agreement. Successfully hunting a stag requires most, but not necessarily all the hunters in the tribe assuming that the tribe is big enough and the hunters competent enough, among other parameters. There has to be a threshold but the level of this threshold, or tipping point, is not important for the current normative account. A society is at equilibrium when a large enough number of individuals behave in certain, socially accepted way; a society is successful, when a large enough majority adopt a maximising social welfare strategy.

The stag hunt is a more appropriate type of game to be used in social explanation as it takes into account populations and not just individuals. Their differences are not as great as they seem at first. Repeated interactions between two individuals can be described by the PD game structure. Although strictly speaking the PD game is not iterated, its pay-off structure can be used to examine repeated interactions. In this case benefit from future interactions becomes important. So, a PD game where future pay-off is important enough to affect rational deliberation can yield similar results to the stag hunt. Assuming that individuals are not rational in the narrow economic definition, but rather are rational in a social sense, as described in Chapters 1 and 2 and later in this chapter, then the PD and the stag hunt are very close in describing individual behaviour, social interactions and social equilibria.

The "shadow of the future" (ibid: 4) is about the importance attributed to future interactions. Agents who believe it is important to maximise pay-offs in future interactions, are more likely to cooperate in the present. Those who perceive interactions as repeated will see the obvious advantage of participating in cooperative interactions. Also known as "future discount factor", the shadow of the future is a central idea in repeated games. The smaller the future discount factor, the greater the importance of future interactions for the players. In a PD type game for instance, if the two prisoners expect to be arrested and to be offered the same deal again, it is more likely that they will keep silent. The shadow of the future makes cooperation rational and the games of the stag hunt and the PD are similar. However, similar is not same; "[t]he shadow of the future has not solved the problem of cooperation in the prisoner's dilemma; it has transformed it into the problem of cooperation in the stag hunt" (ibid: 6). Skyrms's work focuses on social interactions but as a result, time becomes important. Chapter 4 focuses on time, but the premise is similar with Skyrms's; sociability leads to intertemporality. Individuals interacting in a social environment, and being aware of the social nature of interactions, will eventually incorporate time in their deliberation. When a rational agent considers the impact of social groups and structures in her rational deliberation, considering time, is only the next logical step. This is the case because social interactions, unlike one to one interactions, cannot be easily assumed to be taking place instantaneously – even theoretically. When an agent has many interlocutors, time and space must be incorporated in the discussion. A one to one interaction can be theoretically assumed to be taking place simultaneously or successively but in an environment where time is affecting results. Assuming that agents are spread within a social group, similar to Skyrms, makes it implausible to argue or even assume that information about interlocutors' behaviour is conveyed instantly.

Drawing connecting lines between the two games is important because it shows two things. First, that cooperation in a two person game can be examined in a group context and its likelihood is influenced by broader social dynamics; second, that the premises and assumptions underlying game theoretical models, not just the games' formal description, are valuable. By extension, individual behaviour can be examined in conjunction with collective behaviour with the help of a theory of cultural evolution and rationality can be reconciled with social interactions.

Game theory can describe strategic interaction over generations. When individuals of the original generation cooperate, they will produce cooperators who will in turn cooperate eventually reaching a group or society where cooperation is the norm. Put differently, social contract games are played over generations. The game played by the original generation of a population affects the eventual equilibrium point reached after several generations. Whether this will be a cooperative or a non-cooperative equilibrium depends on whether the founding generation cooperated or defected. Therefore, the stability of the social contract depends on interactions that took place several generations earlier.

Skyrms analyses how depending on factors that will be discussed later, both stag and hare hunting equilibria, are possible and will be stable once established. Despite the stag hunt equilibrium being optimal, individuals can opt to hunt hare which is also an equilibrium. Gauthier offers reasons for which constrained maximisation is rational but Skyrms's limits his argument to explaining how equilibria evolve. Although they are very similar in that they distinguish between two types of behaviour whose rationality depends on one's neighbours, the latter account more clearly focuses on including and explaining social structures. Moreover, Skyrms's explanatory model is based on the co-evolution of strategies and social structures which in turn depend on the relative location of cooperators and defectors, the possibility of communication and the subsequent association.

Functionalism and conventional behaviour

Individuals' actions can, and usually do, have implied and unintended functions for a given society (Martin and McIntyre, 1994; Levin, 2010). The following section is an examination of the extent to which functional analysis of social structures can be incorporated in the rational choice theory framework presented earlier. Functional explanation will serve as a stepping stone in reconciling the methodological individualism of game theory with the holism of social theory.

The typical example by which functionalism is usually discussed in the literature is the rain dance. Although it does not bring rain, it serves as a mechanism of reinforcing social cohesion (ibid). In similar vein, Hollis (1994) uses a termite colony to discuss functionalism; each termite behaves in a certain way because otherwise the colony would collapse. Functional analysis focuses on society as a whole, ignoring individuality. Society needs the rain dancer and the termite colony needs the termites to keep behaving as they do in order for established social structures to be sustainable. For functionalism, individuals matter in the sense that their social role matters.

The actions of the individuals in a society are explained through the purpose they serve for society and not in terms of individual benefit. Thus, functionalism and rationality are found at opposite sides of the spectrum in terms of individualistic and holistic approaches to social explanation. However, given the flexible understanding of rationality presented previously, individual rationality can be reconciled with functionalism. The rain dancer behaves rationally whether he believes his dance will bring rain or he realises he merely fulfils a social function; by fulfilling his social role, he also maximises his utility. Maximisation in this case can either be rainfall, or one's ability to be a contributing member of a social group. The rain dancer maximises his individual utility by playing a social role, which is essential for social cohesion. Mainstream economics asserts that a rational agent adopts strategies that will bring the highest benefit, assuming that the agent has full information and understanding of his strategies and his environment. In the current account, it is not important why an agent behaves as he does, as long as his behaviour maximises his utility. If a termite carries food to the nest and as a result he has enough food for the winter, that does not mean that the individual termite has undertaken a process of rational deliberation. However, the individual termite is better off as a result of his and his colony's actions and as such, his behaviour can be seen as rational. Similarly, the rain dancer behaves according to an established social convention of behaviour in order to retain his role in the social structure that maximises his share of the cooperative surplus, while also maximising his individual benefit. In this respect, functional analysis can be used in conjunction with rational behaviour and game theory to analyse interactions in a dynamic environment (McClennen, 1990; Martin and McIntyre, 1994).

Functional behaviour supports conventions of behaviour, in a similar way to that in which the termites support the sustainability of their colony. Individuals do not need to act intentionally for the stability of a convention but their actions are essential for its stability. Social conventions arise from repeated pairwise interactions between rational agents and over time acquire force similar to the force of the rain dance. Hence, conventions are dynamic and depend on agents' strategies that adapt to changes in their environment. According to this understanding, a convention does not always need to satisfy a specific goal in society; it may be the result of unintended actions, serving an implied function for social cohesion.

Social rationality

Rationality is linked to and depends on society and social interactions as well as time. Rational agency needs to be defined in terms of a social and time framework and as such, it is modular (Gaus, 2011); a rational agent follows a life-plan for maximisation and acts accordingly. However, doing so does not restrict choice, it merely gives it context. Modular rationality is to be seen as general guidelines rather than a detailed plan for maximisation. Hence, rational strategy is subject to revisions as during one's lifetime more information becomes available. In a game theoretical framework, agents re-think their plan at decision nodes and either continue on their original plan or adopt a new strategy. In other words, rational agents learn from experience (Young, 2001). Rationality is as much an individualistic concept as it is a collective one. It is endogenous in that each agent decides how to best achieve her goals and exogenous in that individual rational deliberation is influenced by one's social surroundings.

The account of social rationality proposed here is based on two assumptions. First, interactions are interdependent and repeated. Humans interact in a social environment and as a result each interaction relates to another. When agent A interacts with agent B, and at the same time interacts with agent C, his experience from one interaction is transferred to the other. Therefore, A is a link between the two set of interactions or among all interactions in which he participates; the agent is also a means of information transmission. A's behaviour is affected by the outcome of each interaction and by the behaviour of B, C and so on. If A and B are strangers and they do not expect to meet again, their interaction history affects their disposition and therefore their strategies in their interaction. In this context, A and B never interact in an one-off interaction, as they perceive every interaction part of a continuum of interactions, or else part of social life. This describes a version of rationality-based indirect reciprocity. However, the current account emphasises the importance of the social group dynamics and the socially established behaviour equilibria as opposed to the need to keep track of others' past behaviour.

Second, assumptions about agent memory and information availability are necessary to support the suggested account of rationality. Rational strategies depend on the available information. Within a given social group, information can spread through imitation and communication and thus, everyone has roughly equal information, which is not to be confused with complete information. Rational agents with access to similar information should adopt similar strategies.

Furthermore, it is plausible to assert that each agent has roughly the same memory. It does not have to be full memory of every decision in the interaction's history, but "each individual remembers a general experience" (Sugden, 2004: 60). This memory creates a disposition to act accordingly in the future, that is either reinforced or undermined by one's social environment. Most agents in the given group should have similar memory of the common history and adapt strategies accordingly. Furthermore, information availability is not restricted to a social group but can be spread throughout groups and societies, thus dealing with the issue of 'intruders' (Skyrms, 2004). A stranger in a group cannot take advantage of the social dynamics as his behaviour can be known more widely and thus affect his future interactions.

A rational agent as described above is assumed to have access to roughly the same information as her neighbours, a similar capacity to remember past interactions and evaluate her environment which leads to developing similar maximising strategies for a given environment. Thus, the definition of rational behaviour depends on social environment and maximising strategies are bound by environmental constraints. Therefore, rational agency is socially bound and defined.

In game theory agents' strategies are subject to change in similar ways that in real life people's behaviour and beliefs change. A strategy shift can occur when the amount of information a player possesses changes or when a player's history changes as the game evolves. A player's history is being enriched continuously as the players interact in a game. And thus, her strategies and objectives change accordingly. In that respect rational behaviour is not set. In a dynamic context strategies and behaviour depend on or at least are affected by environmental parameters.

As the number and disposition of the players in the game change, rational players' strategies have to adapt to the changing environment. Robinson Crusoe is a commonly used example for homo-economicus; Crusoe is constrained by his environment, his skills and the time he has available in his efforts to maximise his utility in the given environment. He makes the most out his environment, skills and time to achieve as high an utility as possible. All this changes when man-Friday appears turning the example into one of strategic interactions. Crusoe's rational deliberation and rational strategies must adapt and change to the new social environment (Hollis, 1994). An agent has to shift her behaviour depending on whom she interacts with, the frequency, and the salience of her interactions, in addition to considering the natural environment, her skills and time. In a group of non-cooperators, the rational response would be non-cooperation whereas in a group of cooperators, cooperation will maximise a player's utility. Therefore, a rational response is always dependent on the expected behaviour of others. From these premises it is safe also to conclude that when environmental parameters remain stable, rational agents have no reason to alter their strategies.

Therefore, environmental parameters such as the number of interacting agents and their history are central to the present understanding of rationality. The strategies dictated by rationality depend on the game parameters. In this respect, rationality is still central to the argument and the basic premises of traditional game theory remain the same. Individuals want to maximise their utility and are able to learn and adjust to changes. Furthermore, a player's environment becomes a central concept in analysing rational behaviour. The interactions between Crusoe and man Friday are the first of their kind, given that they live on an isolated island. Their repeated interactions will give rise to habits of behaviour. These habits will replace rational analysis of the possible choices at each decision node. Therefore, without abandoning rationality, Crusoe and Friday will stop behaving strategically in their set environment. Their behaviour will be determined by the rational decisions they made at the beginning of their interaction. They will be based on their interaction history and follow patterns of behaviour, without deliberating rationally. Social conventions, developed as a result of their repeated interactions in a stable environment, will replace their rational decision making process. Over the course of infinitely repeated interactions, they behave so as to serve a social function which is essential for the continuation of interactions. But this does not mean they lose their capacity to think rationally. Rational agents have the option to follow the – rationally established – convention or to defect. Conventions are dynamic in that they are affected by the environmental parameters. Therefore, when the number of players changes, convention equilibria will have to shift.

If there is a new arrival on the island, he will also seek to maximise his utility and make the most of the situation. In essence however he has two options: follow the established convention or abstain and interact according to traditional rational choice theory. The maximising behaviour would be to take advantage of the achievements made by the two original inhabitants. In this context where the island's limited resources can be divided among a small group of individuals, if the new arrival decided not to follow the established convention but instead managed to interact following new rules dictated by his rationality, the outcome would be similar to the outcome of the interactions within the convention. Since the environment is set, rational interactions would lead to the same outcome – the establishment of similar conventions of behaviour. Maximising strategies are similar since the environmental parameters have not changed.

Newcomers on the island will follow the established conventions unless they find a new way to achieve the same maximising outcome. The conventions established by the interactions of a first generation of rational individuals will hold for the following generations. In this view, social conventions are the result of a Nash equilibrium point. Those who decide that it is in their best interest not to adhere to the existing rules will bear two different costs: First is the cost of rationally analysing their best strategy. The more complicated the society in which they live, the higher this cost. Second is the cost of finding agents who would be willing to interact with them and pay the cost of being excluded from the established convention. It might seem that there are two kinds of rationality: one pointing towards behaving conventionally and another dictating defection. However, what differs is the amount of information and the perception of the environment. Provided the environmental parameters are the same, both behaviours will lead to a Nash equilibrium. The non-behaviour however will be more costly and time consuming.

Crusoe and Friday have not entered into a contract in the traditional way. Their common understanding of what should be done and their common aim (to maximise their utility) implicitly bind them. This agreement however does not have the form of mutual obligation but of egoistic maximisation, as one needs the other in order to survive. This informal contract then takes the form of the convention that is adhered to by new arrivals (or future generations), whose behaviour is described by their structural roles: they behave according to the role they occupy in society and by doing so, they maximise their utility without necessarily intending to do so. This however does not presuppose rational deliberation; agents behaving like that can fit in with the concept of rationality as presented above. By fulfilling her social role responsibilities she maximises her utility. Rational deliberation reinforces the behaviour that is promoted by society. Agents maximise in the long term and not in each decision node. What matters is that there is maximisation at the end of each interaction or set of interactions. In this context, homo sociologicus (Rescorla, 2011) is a rational agent taking into account environmental parameters and how they change.

Following Sugden (2004), whether we drive on the left or right is a matter of habit and a result of a social evolution process. Rational deliberation shows that it is rational to conform with the established convention. And the convention has been established in the first place as the result of pairwise interactions between rational agents. This applies not only to dove-hawk type of games; in a prisoner's dilemma game cooperation is the only Pareto efficient solution. But the Nash equilibrium depends on what the other player is disposed to do. In a repeated prisoners' dilemma game between Crusoe and Man Friday, the Nash equilibrium will be cooperation. The same applies for small groups where free-riders are known. Therefore, in small groups where complete information and memory of the history of the game are known, cooperative conventions will be established. Even in cases when the opponent is not known, it pays to cooperate as it is more probable that the opponent will follow the convention as well. Rational individuals will choose to interact with agents within their group. When they interact with agents outside their group, they will be able to know the reputation of the group. And if they come across a free-rider, his behaviour will become known in both groups, making the cost of free-riding even higher. Therefore, small groups do not necessarily restrict the number of interactions of the possible agents one can interact with.

The evolution of interactions and social structures leads to the creation of conventions. In this story individual rationality does not play a central role; agents follow the conventions as they have evolved through repeated interactions. Before that, social structures define strategy sets. In order to show that this social dynamics approach can complement the individualistic account of constrained maximisation, we will have to show how agents who accept conventions that are the result of social processes are also rational. Skyrms shows how the creation of a cooperative or non-cooperative structure depends on one's neighbours and their predispositions. In this framework, it is rational to be cooperative when you are surrounded by cooperators. A free-rider will be punished by social exclusion and his gains from defecting are much smaller than the costs of social exclusion. Non-cooperative interactions do not produce a cooperative surplus. Groups of non-cooperators then do worse than groups of cooperators. The rational agent in a group of cooperators will choose to participate in cooperative interactions in order to increase her pay-off. Non-cooperative groups will thus mutate into cooperative groups. When we allow for rational deliberation, in Skyrms's story, cooperation is the rational strategy.

The above understanding of functional and conventional rationality emphasizes instrumental rationality without departing significantly from traditional definitions. Rational individuals still deliberate on how to maximise. However, they also follow the established conventions for a great proportion of their decisions. Since this maximises their utility and they have the rational capability to adhere to the predefined rules or not, they are still rational maximisers. Furthermore, rational agents have the capacity to reflect and apply backward induction on their strategies and their behaviour in relation to social conventions. They have the capacity to compare the outcome of conventional and non-conventional behaviour at the end of a set of interactions.

In a sense rational, utility maximising individuals have reasons to behave like the termites to an extent: do as they are expected by social conventions but without abandoning rational deliberation about whether their behaviour yields the best possible outcome. Individual rational behaviour can have long-term unintended implications and showing that individual rationality can coexist with explanations of collective behaviour is essential before discussing how rational behaviour can be examined within a social context.

Constrained maximisation as conventional rationality

Rationality must consider the impact of society and as such, it cannot be an exclusively individualistic concept. In a social-evolutionary context, agents within a social convention will constrain their maximisation by behaving conventionally. Should social conventions of constrained maximisers yield higher utility, they will spread and replace lower utility alternatives. Constrained maximisation as introduced in Morals by Agreement is problematic since it requires disposition translucency which is an unrealistic stipulation.

Constrained maximisation is based on the assumption that dispositions are translucent. When an agent knows that the agent he interacts with is going to constrain her maximisation, then he will form the disposition to constrain his maximisation as well. And in this case, constrained maximisation is rational. Ideally, dispositions would be transparent, so that constrained maximisers would only interact with agents of similar disposition and thus constrained maximisation would be a maximising strategy. It is vital then that "the straightforward maximiser and the constrained maximiser both appear in their true colours" (Gauthier, 1986: 173). Gauthier rightly asserts that translucency is more realistic than transparency. It is more realistic to assume that actors can guess others' disposition at a high probability than that dispositions are just known. However, there is no argument as to how translucency comes about and how it can be achieved in the real world. The fact that translucency is more realistic than transparency does not necessarily make it realistic enough. "[T]he ability to detect dispositions of others must be well developed in a rational CM" (Gauthier, 1986: 181). It is obviously rational for one to practice detecting dispositions, but how is this ability developed? The problem of guessing others' disposition remains.

The visibility of one's disposition is not, in the social rationality account, as much of a problem as it is in Gauthier's constrained maximisation. Accepting that agents can be rational within a social equilibrium, we will have to give a plausible account of how they trust others to constrain their maximisation. Within a convention that defines the boundaries of behaviour everyone acts accordingly. Everyone behaves as if everybody else will behave conventionally. Thus, agents act conventionally and also rationally when deliberating about whether to defect. Therefore, dispositions become a secondary issue, despite this account being very close conceptually to the rationality of constrained maximisation in a group of constrained maximisers. In a social setting individuals can look at others' past interactions in order to make an educated guess about their future behaviour.

Looking at the stag hunt game reinforces the argument. If the pay-off of hunting hare is 3 and the pay-off of cooperatively hunting stag is 4, everybody would hunt stag when they expect everybody else to do the same. This brings us back to the problem of disposition translucency. Assuming that a stag hunt was possible during the first interaction, those who decided to hunt hare will not be accepted in the next stag hunt. After repeated hunts, the individual pay-off from hunting stag will be greater than the pay-off from hunting hare. This would result in stag hunting becoming the dominant strategy. If stag hunting were impossible at the beginning, this society would reach a hare hunting equilibrium. It is up to the individual rationality of its members then, to imitate a more successful society that has established a stag hunt. Similarly, in a repeated prisoners' dilemma, if one defects the first time the game is played, then it should be expected that the second time both will defect and the game will result in a non-cooperative equilibrium. If a cooperative equilibrium had been established instead, both would be maximising their utility in a repeated game.

In discussing constrained maximisation, Gauthier says: "The just person [...] has internalized the idea of mutual benefit" (Gauthier, 1986: 157). The just person though has been shown to be a rational person who complies with the principle of minimax relative concession. Constrained maximisation is therefore based on the idea that rational agents have made fairness part of their rational deliberation. Put differently, Gauthier stipulates that rational agents have made morality part of their decision making process when they interact with similarly disposed agents. Similarly, the just person conforms to conventional rules as she wants to avoid deliberation costs and exclusion from the conventions that surround her. Repeated interactions within a small population ensure free-riders are found and excluded, and thus knowing each other dispositions is not a central condition of constrained maximisation. Interactions evolve as individuals grow, learn and gain experience and this has an impact on the way individuals interact. Repeated interactions create dynamics that have an effect on the possible strategies and outcomes of a game, such as trust and social bonds. Gauthier argues that an action is rational when the final outcome of a series of interactions is maximising, irrespective of the outcome of each single action. Constrained maximisation implicitly describes long-term maximisation, which is more sensible as the result of a process that considers social dynamics and the social context.

In a social dynamics analysis, disposition visibility is not essential. The fact that cooperators or non-cooperators form groups that follow certain conventions makes it highly unlikely that these conventions will be broken. What is more important, it makes it very costly to break these conventions. Rational reflective individuals can see how breaking an equilibrium will only pay in the short term. Within their group they will be punished by being excluded from future conventions. A population will only abandon the status-quo for a Pareto superior equilibrium point. Therefore, the behaviour inside this population can only change through imitation of a more successful interaction structure.

Rationality as understood through constrained and straightforward maximisation in reference to the dispositions of the population, is very close to the understanding of rationality in social context. Gauthier implicitly takes a holistic perspective when defending constrained maximisation: "A straightforward maximiser [...] must expect to be excluded from cooperative arrangements..." (Gauthier, 1986: 187). It is rational to constrain maximisation in a population of constrained maximisers. Rationality thus depends on the strategies employed by the whole population and not just one individual. Therefore, a cooperative society is not always the outcome of rational interactions.

The social account of rationality presented in this chapter does not necessarily favour cooperation. This can be only one of the possible outcomes. A non-cooperative equilibrium is as likely. This is in agreement with Gauthier's argument that justice is only rational in a society of constrained maximisers; "[i]n a world of Fooles, it would not pay to be a constrained maximiser" (Gauthier, 1986: 183). A society based on constrained maximisation achieves a higher Pareto efficiency point and therefore groups of constrained maximisers do better.

5 Intertemporality

As a consequence of repeated interactions within a social context, intertemporal choice becomes a core element of the present argument. Rational agents have to consider time, as well as interlocutors' strategies over time, in adopting maximising strategies. Intertemporality draws from the literature on dynamic choice and rationality and is intrinsically linked with sociability. In a social setting all interactions are repeated and likely non-random. Repetitiveness introduces time dynamics. In a social setting rational agents very rarely have to make decisions in a static environment; the number and disposition of potential interlocutors may change and other parameters affecting one's decision are also subject to change. Therefore, an account of dynamic rationality is needed in order to examine rational agency and decision-making over time. This approach touches issues of rational commitment (Coleman and Morris, 1998) and on Parfit's (1984) work on two levels: First, there is the tension between rational maximisation in one-off interactions and in repeated interactions. Second, there is the issue of individual identity over the long term; a rational agent's preferences can change dramatically over her life to the extent that we cannot be thinking of her as one person, in the context of rational agency. As such, rationality over the long term is linked to sociability and social rationality and the justifiability of other-regarding behaviour. In the same manner that individuals from their rational strategies informed and constrained by their environment, a single agent adapts her strategies over her lifetime as her environment changes. What is rational at time t, is not necessarily rational at time t+n. Whether rational strategies and the social equilibrium adapt because of a single person adapting to her environment or because of new individuals entering society does not affect the presented account of rationality. Economic accounts of rational agency will not allow maximisation over a series of interactions. However, intertemporality allows interactions without immediate maximisation, and as a result allows for behaviour that meets the morality criteria. Introducing time, in addition to sociability, to rational deliberation, qualifies the mainstream account of rational choice; a rational agent is one who makes the most of her situation given the information available and the social environment. This is a departure from the homo-economicus model but the two approaches share one significant element; the idea that individuals are mutually unconcerned. Selfishness remains the main assumption of the characterisation of human behaviour and since the aim here is to examine the links between rationality and morality, self-interested behaviour is the most important aspect of homo-economicus.

Intertemporal rationality

Contractarianism solves the problem of compliance by using rational agreement as its foundation. Hence, the problem shifts to intertemporal rationality. An action A is rational at time t, but does this mean that it is also rational at time t+n? Not necessarily; this is one of the weaknesses of the proposed account: rational agents might change their minds, should new information become available, or should their preferences simply change. In this case, interactions with similarly disposed agents might replace the old ones, and a new social contract might be tacitly agreed upon. Although this account is weak in terms of its long term stability, it addresses problems of compliance and its static approach to rational agency. Compliance is only expected when it is rational in the current social environment, which is subject to change. If the environment changes, then new strategies may become rational, and all rational interlocutors, with access to similar information, should be able to appreciate the need for change and the fact that compliance to previously made agreements cannot be expected. This is similar to Skyrms's account, presented in Chapters 1 and 2, that discussed evolving social equilibria depending on the strategies employed by the individuals making up the social group. A stag hunt is only rational if there is an adequate number of stag hunters in the group; if the composition of the group changes, hare hunting might be the maximising strategy and rational agents must adapt. Compliance with the stag hunting social convention becomes irrational.

The importance of time in rational deliberation and interactions has been discussed in the literature, primarily in game theoretical terms. In addition to Skyrms, Ken Binmore has developed an evolutionary account of the social contract (Binmore, 1998). More recently and less formally, in *Against Empathy* Bloom (2018) argues that empathy causes people to overestimate present and underestimate future costs and by implication, benefit. The importance of time in social interactions among rational or moral agents has been well-documented and discussed and as such the present account is not innovative in this respect. It is however innovative in that intertemporality is used as building block for rational agency and social interactions that lead to moral outcomes. In the absence of intertemporal considerations, if for instance agents do not care about the future the argument for the morality of rational interactions does not hold. One must care about one's future benefit to sufficiently to be willing to constrain present maximisation. The case for this has been made in previous chapters, starting with the idea of constrained maximisation that is rational in a social setting with time-conscious agents.

Sociability over time

Human behaviour is characterised by sociability, and social interactions must entail intertemporality. Social interactions include more than two people and as a result it takes time for information about others' interactions to spread and be used in rational deliberation. In addition, in theoretical but especially practical terms interactions within a social groups must take time as interlocutors are not always nearby. As such, rational agency is defined by the dynamic nature of social and intertemporal interactions.

The argument for intertemporality relies on the assumption of sociability; all interactions take place in a social environment. This may sound like a truism, but definitions of instrumental rationality usually ignore the impact of the social environment on rational behaviour. Rational agency, is taken to be the mutually unconcerned behaviour that aims at utility maximisation. Since all interactions take place in a social setting, individual behaviour and interaction outcomes can be known to the social group.

Sociability leads to repetitiveness. Given information availability about interactions that is made possible within social groups all interactions are non-random since one's past behaviour can be known and one's interlocutors can adjust their strategies. In this respect, all interactions are repeated. If for example an agent cooperates in an interaction represented by a Prisoner's Dilemma (PD) game, then she is likely to be expected to cooperate in similar interactions in the future and thus, attract similarly disposed interlocutors.

Repetitiveness follows from sociability and is the basis for intertemporality. Accepting that all interactions are repeated means that we must also accept the dynamic and intertemporal nature of human interactions. Agents are still assumed to be instrumentally rational, but their rational deliberation, preferences and rational choices are affected by the given social environment. This account of rationality is then close to bounded rationality; rationality here is bound by one's social environment. Social environment serves both as constraining rational deliberation as well as a mechanism for information spreading. Past interactions inform a rational agent's deliberation about strategy adoption. Different social environments promote different behaviours and as such, maximising strategies depend on the given social environment. Therefore, cooperating in a PD game can be rational should a given social group is made up mostly by cooperators. Similarly, defection can be rational if defecting is the dominant strategy in the group. However, cooperative groups achieve higher social welfare and as such, in the long run social groups that promote cooperation can be expected to expand, taking over groups whose social equilibrium is defection. Intertemporal choice is a logical conclusion of sociability. Within a social environment, all interactions are repeated and all choice is intertemporal.

As such, it is rational to adopt future-orientated strategies. Those agents who do not, find themselves in suboptimal social equilibria; having assumed rationality, they must choose to change their strategies. As a result, a small future discount factor becomes an essential element of the characterisation of rational agency; within an environment of social and therefore, repeated interactions, reputation and interaction history become essential elements of rational deliberation.

Based on the above, rational agency, and by extension human agency more generally, has to be social and intertemporal. This is true even when discussing instrumental rationality, which is usually approached from an individualistic and reductionist angle, assuming, or asserting that deliberation and interactions take place in a social, timeless vacuum (Elster, 1982). The proposed approach argues for an account of agency that combines elements of homo-economicus and homo-sociologicus. Agents are mutually unconcerned, utility maximisers, but at the same time they are affected by their social environment and the effect of time in their strategic deliberation. This paradigm synthesis becomes unavoidable once we accept that interactions are social and repeated. Ultimately, rational agency must be social and intertemporal.

Morality and mutual advantage

A theory of morality as mutual advantage must give an account of why rational individuals should care for others, especially the weak, even when there is no immediate benefit in so doing. The core of any theory of morals has to include a justification for helping those who cannot reciprocate. The outcome of such moral behaviour would lead to a social equilibrium that meets the requirements for social justice. Theories of justice as mutual advantage and practical rationality entail the notion of mutual unconcern. Rational agents maximise their own utility functions without having an interest in the maximisation of others or put differently "utility functions are to be defined independently of one another" (Morris in Vallentyne, 1991: 81). The assumption of mutual unconcern is an essential requirement for rational agency and in turn for a discussion of justice as mutual advantage. If not, one could just assume that humans are empathetic, benevolent and mutually concerned and therefore justice would be the outcome of any social interaction. In the account of justice as mutual advantage, which is the one discussed here, rational agents should only participate in interactions as long as it maximises their own utility irrespective of what happens to others. The essence of the assumption of rationality is that agents have to be self-regarding and only interact with others when it helps them promote their own interests. Therefore, it is obvious that combining justice as mutual advantage and participation in interactions without direct mutual benefit can be problematic.

It is very difficult if not completely impossible to give an account of why conventions of caring for the weak were established in the first place. A very likely and plausible explanation can be that they serve as insurance. As mentioned in the previous section, it is rational to care for the disabled, as well as the very old, as a form of insurance which will be realised if one becomes very old or disabled. Despite the difficulty of giving an empirical account of how such conventions have emerged, it is a fact that most modern societies have a justification and a method for including no contributors, at least to some extent. Although it would have been very useful to be able to give a justification based on rationality of how modern social conventions include severely disabled infants for instance, it is not as important as recognising that this is an established convention. The fact that conventions of helping the weak have survived and become established social norms indicates that they do serve a purpose that is socially beneficial. However, this is just an indication, albeit an important one; societies have moved from excluding the weak, to discriminating against them, to trying to include them as equals in the social contract. Therefore, we can claim that social cohesion and efficiency are not threatened by including those who are significantly weaker than the average. Although the historical development of conventions for the old and the unborn has not been the same, their contractarian justification is.

Power discrepancies between contracting parties refer to differences in the ability to contribute to the cooperative surplus in similar terms. The reasons behind unequal contributions may be the result of differences such as wealth, natural skills or may also have to do with an agent's age, such as the too young or the too old to contribute. Also, significant differences include situations where a potential contracting party is so severely disabled that she cannot be expected to make any contribution at any time. The following discussion will focus on the latter case because it is the most challenging for theories of justice as mutual advantage. If there can be a convincing answer for cases of severely disabled individuals participating in the social contract, then cases of great power differences will be included.

Theories of justice as mutual advantage have been criticised for excluding the vulnerable (Barry, 1991); if the criticism is valid, then it is claimed that they cannot be convincing as theories of justice. However, a theory of justice as mutual advantage does not have to exclude the vulnerable. There are two distinct rational premises for justifying caring for the non-contributors. First, a cooperative surplus is achieved even when there is an interaction with someone too young to contribute, as long as he is expected to contribute in the future. Second, interacting with non-contributors can be seen as insurance and can be justified through a rationale of indirect reciprocity.

A rational agent has reasons to participate in interactions characterised by extreme power inequalities interactions because they require smaller contributions from the powerful party than interactions between equals; an interaction with a weak person requires a contribution that does not have to be the maximum possible but merely proportionate to the contribution of the weak. In this respect, an interaction with someone who cannot contribute as much can still be beneficial although not necessarily maximising. Hence, a rational agent should always choose to interact with someone of roughly equal capabilities. When this is not possible, interacting with someone weaker is also rational in the sense that there can be a cooperative surplus greater than would be through individual production. A handicapped person can still contribute to an interaction though she may not be as productive as an able-bodied individual.

The second rational justification for interacting with the weak is more directly linked to the understanding of social behaviour as conventional behaviour. Caring for the non-contributors can be justified as a form of insurance and a type of indirect reciprocity. Able-bodied individuals care for those who cannot support themselves, expecting that if they find themselves in the same position, others will do the same. These conventions are rational within small groups where free-riding can be identified and punished. And they can have only been established within small groups at first. Viewing modern societies as a collection of smaller social groups where reciprocity and cooperation are rational would mean that there can be a rational justification for this type of behaviour. Moreover, interactions with the weaker are rationally justifiable when we expect a form of indirect reciprocity; we "help those who cannot help themselves, so as to encourage those who can to help us" (Vanderschraaf, 1999: 349). The concept of indirect reciprocity is closely related with multilateral reciprocity; agents who wish to cooperate choose agents who have cooperated in the past and avoid agents who have defected in the past. Sugden (2004) argued that in repeated, n-person Prisoner's Dilemma type games, behaviour is known and therefore free-riding is too costly a strategy to be adopted. Even in this case however, the maximising strategy depends on the strategies the majority of the population adopts; "in a world of nasties, just as in a world of suckers, cooperation never pays" (Sugden, 2004: 125). Multilateral reciprocity, similarly to the Rawlsian notion of indirect reciprocity, calls for agents to cooperate with those who have a history of cooperation and defect when they interact with known defectors. The main premise is that all agents will prefer a cooperative to a non-cooperative equilibrium in a PD type game. However, the PD game distinction need not be exclusive. The value of Sugden's argument lies in the idea that rational agents look at others' past behaviour instead of guessing their disposition of relying on idealistic or metaphysical human traits; this applies to all human interactions and not just those that are possible to be described by a PD game. Even in the two person, one iteration PD game, collective welfare is maximised with cooperation. Cooperative behaviour in n-person, n-iteration games, is self-reinforcing: the greater the number of individuals who cooperate, the better the outcome. Cooperation, despite being costly, produces a greater amount of cooperative surplus, and thus there is more to be distributed. Therefore, it is maximising for most to be at a cooperative equilibrium. Provided that there are enough cooperators, cooperation will be a stable equilibrium.

In real life there is no ring of Gyges and at some point everyone will have to interact with someone who is significantly more powerful than the average. Interactions occur between parties of different power and most agents will find themselves interacting with much more powerful agents, more or less frequently.

A stronger justification for rational agents to interact with those who cannot contribute or cannot contribute as much, is that in the conventional account building a good reputation is vital as well as using these interactions as insurance. One can use interactions where one's benefit is very small or non-existent to boost one's reputation and attract similarly disposed agents. A rational agent who has built a reputation for cooperation or even irrational behaviour will find that it is much easier to convince cooperators to interact with her in interactions with higher than normal benefits. At the same time, she will avoid interactions with agents who have not shown similar behaviour and therefore avoid being taken advantage of. The assumption that interactions are repeated and their history is known ensures that those who have a cooperative history will only cooperate among each other and avoid agents with a history of defection. The repetitiveness assumption also makes it possible to assert that the first stages of a series of interactions are a trial and error process during which interacting agents test the waters by engaging in small benefit and low risk interactions.

In addition, stable conventions have been assumed to build and develop incrementally; low significance interactions are used to build trust among rational agents and as a safety mechanism to make free-riding costly. In this context, someone who has a reputation of not taking advantage of the weak is much less likely to attempt to cheat his equals and be a free-rider and thus, will be more likely to be accepted in a cooperative convention. In the same spirit, a cooperative reputation is not very likely to attract defectors as the low importance and low pay-off of initial interactions, make cooperative interactions too costly for agents who do not aim at establishing long term interactions. This seems to be the strongest case for including severely disabled individuals in the social contract. It is in fact a case of indirect reciprocity. A rational agent who interacts with a disabled can expect to be rewarded by the cooperative surplus of her increased future cooperative interactions. Similarly one can expect to be punished for avoiding interactions or taking advantage of the weak (Vanderschraaf, 2011). Given a reasonable capacity to retain information, rational agents in an established convention will punish those who have exhibited selfish behaviour and reward the altruists.

In conclusion, in all the above cases it is as rational to interact with agents who cannot reciprocate. The account of conventional justice presented here can be problematic on two fronts: first, it does not explain how conventions of interacting with non-contributors emerged in the first place and second, it can be argued that having a reputation for cooperative interactions with non-contributors might harm one by attracting agents who are disposed to defect. The first point is addressed by complementing the account of cooperative reputation with the rationale of helping those in need as a form of insurance policy. Attracting defectors as a result of cooperating with the vulnerable is a danger that is dealt with to a great extent when we take into account the fact that, in the context of repeated interactions, it takes time for a series of cooperative interactions to yield high enough gains so as to make a defector's time and effort worthwhile.

Rational conventions that are based on such inclusive premises are more efficient than exclusive social conventions. Including the severely disabled in the cooperative surplus can only increase the total social output; especially if in the long run the costs for caring for the disabled are minimal by comparison to their potential contributions. Justice as mutual advantage does not have to mean that mutuality is restricted to interactions between two individuals. A rational agent can help someone weaker without expecting an immediate benefit from the specific individual. But having helped him has enhanced her reputation in order to make her future interactions more beneficial. Thus, when we conceive interactions as repeated within a society, indirect reciprocity is a valid argument for the rationality of behaving justly and within the rationale of the theory of justice as mutual advantage. In sum, creating a cooperative reputation leads to more cooperative interactions and thus greater benefits in the long run, but it needs to be viewed in conjunction with cooperation as insurance and whilst taking into account that cooperators will not engage in high benefit interactions with agents who have not proven their intentions.

A final point that needs to be included in the present examination of justice is the concept of desert. Justice is usually discussed in conjunction with desert (Rawls, 2005; Gauthier, 1986). In a just situation everybody gets what she deserves, or in other words, justice provides the regulation according to which a society should decide who deserves what. From the above understanding of justice as mutual advantage it may be concluded that the vulnerable do not receive anything as a result of thinking about what they deserve. In essence they do not deserve to be receivers of the cooperative surplus. However, this does not have to imply that they do not receive anything from the division of the cooperative surplus. Their not being contributors is irrelevant since their participation in the social contract promotes the interests of those who are contributors. Therefore, participation in the social contract does not have to be tied to contribution to the cooperative surplus (Vanderschraaf, 2011).

Inter-conventional justice

The discussion of justice presented in the previous paragraphs has not included an examination of possible conventions of the weak; this is especially relevant when discussing economics and by extension power discrepancies and income inequalities. A moral theory for economic behaviour must have addressed such issues. These have been addressed by implication so far since the discussion has been about rational morality and the importance of rational interactions, which in turn implies that there will be interactions on a roughly equal basis. A rational agent will not participate in interactions with someone who is much more powerful, broadly understood. The same applies with income inequality; a rational agent does not have reasons to interact with someone who is much wealthier or much poorer; rational interaction becomes impossible in this case as the wealthier party would be able to take advantage of the poorer one.

Given extreme inequalities either in skills and wealth or mental and physical capabilities, it is theoretically possible, and a plausible alternative scenario, that rational agents will choose to interact with those of similar strengths. Conventions have been argued to be formed by individuals with access to similar information and thus similar outcomes of rational deliberation. The same can be argued for individuals whose capabilities are characterised by extreme inequalities. If coercion cannot be avoided in cases of extreme inequalities, the weak will choose to interact with agents of similar strength and therefore roughly similar maximising strategies. As a result, there will be social conventions including rational agents of similar strength who achieve optimal outcomes within the given environmental parameters. In this case we can have different types of social conventions within a social contract; social conventions consisting of the weak who simultaneously participate in conventions with stronger agents, should that help them maximise. Conventions of the weak is a realistic proposition, especially if we take into account how in contemporary societies patterns of behaviour change even within the same city. For instance, it is a common phenomenon in contemporary cities to have areas of low crime rates and other areas with very high criminality. These can be seen as different conventions within the boundaries of a single social contract. In this view, interactions between agents of different conventions are possible, though rarely maximising.

Interactions among individuals of different conventions might seem irrational at first view but, as discussed above, inclusive conventions can be more efficient; the same applies when we look at conventions in the context of the social contract and not just individuals in the context of social conventions. Individuals who cannot contribute in one convention can be useful in another; those who are too weak to contribute in a certain environment may be invaluable in a different one when they interact with different individuals.

A more interesting albeit not always as realistic case would be one where rational, non-coercive interactions among individuals of different conventions are not possible. Within an isolated convention rational deliberation can lead to practical outcomes that are incompatible with the rules of other established conventions. Assuming there was no communication between those two conventions in the past but that they can interact in the present, their fundamental differences can make rational interactions impossible. For instance, anthropological and historical evidence shows that European explorers in the 17th century encountered a couple of isolated Polynesian island societies that were not aware of each other. One had a completely peaceful culture of conflict resolution and the other was a typical hierarchical society lead by a warrior elite. The Europeans made the latter aware of the former resulting in the destruction of the peaceful society (Diamond, 2011). In this example, both isolated social contracts can be said to be based on rational conventions, given information and other environmental parameters. However, they had reached extremely different equilibria such that any interaction between them could not be rational. The same probably applies for interactions between the Polynesian and the European culture of the time. Their extreme inequalities in combination with the radically different culture would make rational interactions impossible.

In the modern world there are social states that are considered rational by their members but are viewed as fundamentally irrational by outsiders. Western European states consider many states that do not accept European enlightenment principles as irrational and vice versa. Similarly, within societies there are localised conventions of behaviour can be too different to make rational interactions a realistic possibility. It is obvious that in their circumstances one cannot rely on the rationality of individuals or on conventions for addressing conflicts of interests. This is even more true when between conventions there are significant power and cultural differences. Avoiding interactions is a solid idea theoretically, but not always feasible. Therefore, in cases like the above a third party enforcer may be necessary.

The notion that a third party is needed to solve problems between rational actors that cannot reach agreement is of course nothing new. A form of government intervention is needed, and in some cases is essential, when differences in conventional rationality are too great for an agreement to be reached. This does not have to mean that all differences are reconcilable or that an arbitrator is always needed. It is possible that differences are so extreme that there can be no meaningful method of interaction even with an impartial arbitrator. Furthermore, stable conventions cannot be altered significantly within short periods of time and therefore any government is powerless when its policies collide with the established conventions. The fact remains that impartial arbitrators cannot be ideal agents disconnected from reality and from the social conventions and structures that appointed them in the first place. Therefore, their behaviour should also be described by the conventional account and is limited and bounded by existing social structures. In cases of extreme inequalities like the two island societies above, an impartial arbitrator is not a more plausible solution than the one offered by the conventional account. Extreme inequalities meant that there is a possibility that there can be no agreement on a third party enforcer making coercion or abstention from interactions the only viable alternatives.

6 Information symmetry

Information availability is essential for rational behaviour. As a result of sociability and intertemporality, information spreads. The argument made in this chapter relies conceptually on the previous two chapters on the importance of social interactions and time for rational interactions. Within societies or social groups experience of previous interactions becomes common knowledge and therefore, rational agents adopt similar strategies as they have similar experiences and access to similar information. The basis of this understanding is that behavioural equilibria are the result of information availability. In turn, these equilibria of social behaviour are structurally similar to social conventions. In addition to the mainstream literature on information and social conventions and structures including Lewis, Sugden and Skyrms, established social conventions can also been seen to serve as mechanisms or information transmission and reinforcement. As a result, the discussion on information availability includes an examination of rational agency and social conventions, and the impact of information availability on rational agency and the stability of social conventions and social norms of behaviour. Social interactions within social structures lead to information equality. Information equality does not necessarily have to mean that all interlocutors have access to the same information; rather it means that rational agents from the same social environment, have roughly the same information. Social structures preserve memory of past interactions and hence, facilitate maximising behaviour. For instance, queuing is different in the UK, Italy and China despite the fact that the basic principle is the same. Individuals of the respective societies have an internalised understanding of what they are supposed to do when forming a queue and when a queue is required, although explicit and specific information on queuing is rarely if ever formally conveyed.

Cultural evolution is about changes of social conventions that lead to changes in the social contract; in addition, it encompasses changes in the available information and its processing. Hence, cultural evolution is intrinsically linked with information availability and communication. Rational capabilities cannot be assumed to change over time, but rational deliberation yields different outcomes as the available information is being enriched with past experiences. Cultural evolution depends on the available information, or put differently "[c]ulture is information stored in people's heads, which can be transmitted among individuals" (Gigerenzer, 2002: 2).

Especially in a cultural evolutionary context, information availability has to be taken into consideration in accessing rational behaviour; available information determines rational strategies and as a result, individuals in similar cultures will adopt similar strategies that are maximising. Therefore, cultural evolution to a great extent refers to information availability, which in turn is essential for rational deliberation. Information increases as our history becomes longer and the means for its storage and transmission become more efficient and reliable. Modern people have been able to make better decisions because of the fact that they know more than people in the past, "if progress is real...[it is] because we are born to a richer heritage" (Durant, 2010: 102). Hence, we can claim that the accumulation of knowledge works to our advantage as history evolves. Technological developments and social changes have been making the spreading of this knowledge increasingly easier and therefore have been affecting the outcomes of rational deliberation.

Location, communication, association

The importance of "spatial structure, location and local interaction" (Skyrms, 2004: 15) is paramount for the theory of rational morality presented here. The relative location of interlocutors, influence the social equilibrium reached and the information spreading. The importance of location highlights the importance of sociability and intertemporality discussed previously. A cooperator in a Prisoner's Dilemma (PD) game whose neighbours are defectors will be forced to adapt her strategy and similarly a defector will have to convert to a cooperator in an environment dominated by cooperators – or put differently in a social group that is dominated by constrained maximisers. Individual maximising behaviour depends on one's environment and varies according to one's neighbours.

In this respect, and following Skyrms (2004) we can distinguish between interactions with neighbours and interactions with strangers. A rational individual adjusts her strategies by imitating successful strategies in her neighbourhood. In both cases strategies converge towards those that are maximising; agents who maximised in the first iteration will follow the same strategy in the future, whereas those who did not will change their strategy. Rational agents will cooperate, as long as they prefer the cooperation outcome to the current status. The current status is the point of disagreement. Therefore, an agreement will be reached if and only if the interlocutors' utility is greater after the agreement is reached than before. Interactions with neighbours converge faster whereas interactions with strangers depend on the original spatial arrangements. When interacting with strangers almost 60 percent of simulations lead to a 50-50 division while "[f]air division becomes the unique answer in bargaining with strangers if we change the question to that of stochastic stability in the ultra long run" (ibid: 28).

The establishment of a stable social equilibrium depends on the spatial dynamics of stag and hare hunters. If the majority in the neighbourhood hunts hare then the few stag hunters will be converted, whereas in a neighbourhood or a population of stag hunters, a single hare hunter will change the equilibrium from all hunt stag to all hunt hare. Hare hunting is a risk free strategy as it does not require cooperation and thus it pays off irrespective of the behaviour of others (Hofbauer and Sigmund, 1998). A hare hunter surrounded by stag hunters will change his behaviour next time they bargain. His close neighbours though, will also change to hare hunting. Therefore, after several interactions, hare hunting will be the equilibrium. In terms of interactions between strangers hare hunting has a replication effect on the whole population. "Hare hunting is contagious" (ibid: 36) and eventually a single hare hunter may change the social equilibrium.

The unambiguous conclusion is that "local interaction makes a difference" (ibid: 40) in equilibrium selection. Social equilibrium selection is affected by whether strategies are being imitated within a neighbourhood or replicated in a population (Bergstrom, 2002). The cornerstone of the above spatial analysis is that social structure and repeated interactions matter as much as individual rationality for rational morality. However, individuals imitate the best available strategy not because of rational deliberation as described in mainstream economic theory, but because of the dynamics in a given population. In any case, there is individual utility maximisation even through a social group analysis. The likelihood that a constrained maximiser will interact with others similarly disposed increases in a social group that consists mostly of constrained maximisers.

Communication follows from location; agents who are spatially near are more likely to communicate and exchange information. In turn, communication, just like location, is essential characteristics of sociability, intertemporality and ultimately information equality. Provided that communication before an interaction is possible, a group of cooperators could invade and eventually take over a population of defectors, as communication in this context ensures that future behaviour can be agreed upon within a group of cooperators and enforced within the group through social exclusion. Communication does not solve the problem of compliance in the one-off PD game, but in a stag hunt game it does make a cooperative equilibrium a more likely outcome. Since cooperation is maximising in the long term and individuals can know that others cooperate, it is in everybody's best interest to cooperate. However, costless communication can only have an effect if the cooperators can signal each other using "a secret handshake" (ibid: 66) in order to avoid misinformation. In this context, non-cooperative equilibria can shift to cooperative ones. Thus, the secret handshake is a type of behaviour the precedes interactions and shows that an agent is disposed to cooperate and also that she has cooperated in the past and as a result is aware of the secret handshake. The repetitiveness of interactions enables mechanisms such as the secret handshake to be more plausible and realistic than it might sound at first. Accurately assessing others' future behaviour is possible when we are talking about a social group whose members' past behaviour is known and whose future behaviour can be rewarded or punished, precisely because they are members of the social group.

The possibility of communication before the interaction, just like the relative location of the players, makes a great difference in the outcome. Skyrms (ibid) shows how low or no cost communication can be central in sustaining a cooperative equilibrium provided there is an effective secret handshake. Therefore, communication is as important as location in reaching a maximising equilibrium, a social state where social welfare and individual utility are maximised.

Association in Skyrms (ibid) refers to network formation. Stag hunters who communicate and are located close to each other will create networks of stag hunting equilibria. Therefore, association is based on location and communication which are essential requirements for successful network formation. In addition, association requires agents with learning abilities; successful interactions are repeated (ibid; Skyrms, 2010). Skyrms tells a story of ten strangers exchanging visits.

The greater the pleasure derived from each interaction, the more likely it is that the visit will be repeated. A visit resulting in higher pleasure – or utility – is more likely to be repeated. The contrary applies for a visit that is not pleasant. Moreover, a pleasant visit makes it even more probable that the interaction will be repeated. Adding the concept of memories makes the example more realistic and plausible as it brings the ideal agent of the model closer to the characteristics of real persons. Association is then linked to information availability and location. Agents who have information in the form of memories about past interactions will use this information in making strategy decisions in the future. The nearer a potential interlocutor is, the more likely that successful interactions are repeated. The visits story shows how individuals with no history and free from outside constraints, form bonds as a result of repeated interactions.

Each agent has the opportunity to "look around and if another strategy is getting a better pay-off than his, then he imitates that one" (Skyrms, 2004: 106). This sentence encompasses the central point of the concept of association and the importance of information availability for rational interactions. The agent has the option to imitate more successful strategies and strategies that might have developed in different groups of interaction. Adoption of different strategies will lead to different equilibria and eventually different social contracts. All interactions start from similar initial positions, but the final social contract depends on the agents' choice of strategies, their relative position and the ability to identify each other's intentions accurately. Location, communication and association all play a central role in the evolution of the social contract as presented by Skyrms. A final element of the Skyrms's theory is the co-evolution of location, communication and association; each one develops in parallel with the other and affects it. This further enforces the argument for a dynamic social environment which makes rational morality a possibility. Rational strategies change in time and as the environment changes. However, their relationship is bi-directional, with individual behaviour influencing the environment as well as the other way around.

Individuals who choose their strategy and the agents with whom they will interact, also affect the structure of the game. Therefore, there is a simultaneous process by which maximising strategies develop in parallel with structural changes in social groups. Association is paramount for the theory developed in *The Stag Hunt and the Evolution of the Social Structure* (Skyrms, 2004) because it deals directly with strategy revisions and learning during the game. Co-evolution of structure and strategy adds to association the fact that now agents are able to imitate behaviour that is observed in their social group, even if they have not encountered it; "a player looks around, and if another strategy is getting a better pay-off that his is, he imitates that one" (Skyrms, 2004: 106).

Co-evolution encompasses the previous elements of the theory making it a plausible model for actual social interactions; individuals do change their behaviour when they see someone else doing better or realise that interacting with new individuals will maximise their utility. Humans make friends and enemies based on the pleasure of their interactions as described in the simulations; the more the interactions continue being pleasant, the more the bonds between the interacting agents strengthen, creating social structures that support a type of behaviour. Location, communication and association provide a solid description of human behaviour that is put in a realistic dynamic context with the concept of their co-evolution.

The dynamic analysis of the social contract offered by Skyrms offers a more plausible argument than the static analyses found in mainstream moral contractarianism. Societies are dynamic in that individuals change behaviour and social structures shift accordingly. Social group theory advances the theoretical models of contractarianism since its description of social structures approximates real life societies more accurately than normative theories. Co-evolution exhibits how the equilibrium in a stag hunt game depends on a variety of factors that have to be examined in conjunction in order to be meaningful.

The stag hunt story is a close analogy of reality although it still is an oversimplification of actual social contracts. In reality, one hare hunter (or defectors in the PD game) in a society of stag hunters (or cooperators), will not cause the breakdown of the social structure. However, a critical number of defectors in the population can affect the stability of the social contract. If a stag hunting social contract has been established it cannot be affected by a minority of defectors. However, contagion or free-riding is a problem. When all, or most hunt stag, it pays to free ride by not hunting but participating in the distribution of the successful hunt.

Free-riding behaviour in the long run is "fatal" (Skyrms, 2004: 121). Eventually it can cause the collapse of cooperative equilibria and lead to an all-hunt-hare situation. In a model such as Skyrms's, where social structure and its evolution are central for the argument, free-riding is a maximising strategy if the secret handshake safety mechanism can be bypassed. However, the same applies when the analysis rests exclusively on individual rationality. It is rational for one to benefit from the social output without participating if he can get away with it. Thus, free-riding is central to any discussion of individual rationality in the context of social interactions and poses a significant challenge to the possibility of a rational morality, as it has been exhibited by Hobbes, Hume and Gauthier. Gauthier's constrained maximisation, should it be effective, can provide a more convincing answer to the free-riding problem as it calls for an internalisation of cooperative behaviour (Gauthier, 1986). However, as was discussed in the previous chapter, the concept of internalisation of constrained maximisation is problematic. Free-riding and the possible rational incentives against it will have to be analysed in Chapter 6 where there will be an attempt to show how it is not rational in a repeated interactions framework.

The above discussion continues on the discussion on sociability and intertemporality from the previous two chapters. In addition, Skyrms's work enriches the social contract tradition by incorporating social aspects. There can be a society at a cooperative equilibrium, given enough time, repeated interactions and information availability. Especially the latter is an essential prerequisite for rationality and rational interactions. Rational interactions in turn lead to morality, in a context of social dynamics as well as in pair-wise interactions. Location, communication and association lead to information symmetry and their co-evolution to a social equilibrium that in time is stable and moral.

The ethics of information symmetries

Rational maximisation requires availability of information. Information asymmetries refer to one agent having more information than her interlocutors. Rational deliberation, in this case, leads to different strategies. Rational agents, aiming at maximising utility, in the same environment and with the same constraints will adopt different strategies. All parties attempt to maximise but because of information asymmetries their actions will differ and only those with complete or more accurate information will have maximised at the end of interactions. For rational interactions to take place it is essential that information is freely and equally available to all interlocutors. Within a given social environment, there is a unique strategy that leads to maximisation or, if we relax assumptions of rationality, a specific set of strategies that maximise utility. It becomes essential then that appropriate and accurate information is available to all interlocutors, since the assumption of rational agency ensures that they all have similar capacities to retrieve and use the available information.

Information here refers to information about available strategies and others' history of interactions. The former ensures rationality in that each agent knows the possible actions that are likely to maximise her utility in the given context. The latter ensures that agents can choose their interlocutors; knowing one's past behaviour, increases the probability of accurately predicting her future behaviour. Therefore, a rational agent will chose to interact with agents similarly disposed so as to maximise their respective utilities. An agent who is planning to adopt constrained maximisation strategies will select a similarly disposed interlocutor and avoid straightforward maximisers. Lack of knowledge about others' past makes it more difficult to maximise and more likely that straight-forward maximisers are taken advantage.

Information symmetry is a necessary and essential condition for rational and also for moral interactions. A moral interaction is characterised by mutual advantage and absence of coercion. Any outcome of such interactions is by definition ethical. Given that morality relies on rationality and rational behaviour requires information equality, morality must also require information equality – equality here to mean access to roughly equal amounts and quality of information and it is not to be taken strictly. The important thing is that individuals are able to make choices that are maximising or more importantly, that no interlocutor has access to better or more information. Utility maximisation is only possible when agents have enough information to enable them to make rational decisions. In addition, access to similar information leads to mutually advantageous interactions. Therefore, there is a direct, intrinsic link between information availability, rationality and morality.

Mutual advantage, and by extension moral outcomes requires "fully informed individuals... who are driven to pursue their own self-interest" (Matravers, 2000: 56). Information asymmetries lead to the adoption of different strategies by rational agents. Since the adoption of rational strategies depends on the available information, rational agents with access to different information will most likely adopt different strategies. They make the best decisions based on the information available to them. As such, rational agents may adopt completely different strategies as a result of having access to different information.

Rational interactions and mutual advantage depend on equal rationality, the idea that interlocutors have similar reasoning capacities. In turn, equal rationality relines on equal information. Equal rationality and information symmetry are essential because they are an essential condition for rational interactions; they ensure that rational deliberation leads to maximisation. If information is accurate and adequate a rational agent will make maximising decisions. Should interlocutors have access to different information or different quality of information, the power discrepancies would make mutually beneficial interactions impossible. Given symmetrical information, interlocutors have more to gain by participating in interactions that are mutually beneficial through participating in the "cooperative surplus".

When a rational agent is aware of others' disposition and their disposition is in accordance with hers, it is more likely to interact with them. If they have a history of cooperation, they are more likely to cooperate in the future and thus, it pays to cooperate with them. Although it is impossible for one to predict others' future behaviour with certainty, it is plausible to assert that one can have a good enough knowledge of others' past interactions so as to be able to make educated guesses about their future strategies. If this applies to all members of a group or society, equilibria of acceptable behaviour can be established and sustained. The greater the amount of available information and the equally spread within a social group it is, the more likely it will be that roughly fully informed rational agents will make better choices in selecting whom they interact with. Asymmetrical information leads to exploitation, which it cannot meet any criteria of morality and especially rational morality.

Information availability and rationality

For the alternative account to mainstream economic rationality the main conditions remain the same, but some assumptions of neoclassical economics are relaxed (Heath, 2015). A rational individual is still a utility maximiser with a consistent order of preferences over a set of alternatives. The content of preferences is not examined in assessing the rationality of one's behaviour. In other words, "[w]e do not know what [the rational man] wants...but we know his indifference curves are concave to the origin" (Hollis, 1975: 75). Put differently, the behaviours of both the grasshopper and the ant are rational (Gauthier, 1986). They both maximise their utility, or else their enjoyment, by being heedless and prudent respectively. Provided that imprudence is the result of reflective thinking and its long-term implications are being appreciated, then there is no reason to classify it as irrational. In addition, it is assumed that interactions between rational agents take place in a social context, and thus, are repeated and random.

Interactions between rational, self-interested agents are best represented in a game theoretical framework. In games with the structure of the PD, it pays to defect when the other party's disposition is not known. This is true when the game is not (infinitely) repeated and agents value immediate pay-off higher than their long-term one, that is, they have a high future discount factor. A small discount factor means that agents value future pay-offs highly and in any case not much less than present pay-offs. Therefore, assuming a small future discount factor, rationality dictates to maximise at the end of a series of interactions in a repeated game.

Another assumption of bounded rationality is that all games are infinitely repeated or more realistically, players perceive them as infinitely repeated. When Adam interacts with Eve, in PD type of interaction, and at the same time interacts with a third party, in an interaction described by a game such as hawk-dove, his experience from one game is transferred to the other. Therefore, Adam's behaviour, as informed by the information available to him, is a link between all the interactions in which he participates. Adam's behaviour is affected by the outcome of each interaction and by the behaviour of Eve and his other interlocutors. If Adam and Eve are strangers and they do not expect to meet again, their interaction history will affect their behaviour in their interaction – if Adam has been interacting with defectors in PD type interactions, he is more likely to defect with Eve. Hence, the game they play is affected by the games they had played before they met. Or in other words, the game played between Adam and Eve is a sub-game of all the games they play and their choices are affected by their history. In this context, Adam and Eve never interact in a one-off game, as they perceive every game they play as part of one single large game. All these sub-games are repeated and consequently, mutual cooperation in prisoners' dilemma type of games yields the highest pay-off (Binmore, 1989).

A person who does not maximise her utility immediately, does not necessarily behave irrationally. She still behaves rationally provided that, based on the knowledge and information she has, she believes her actions will maximise her utility. Her actions or set of strategies are confined by environmental parameters that cannot be influenced by her. Therefore, when evaluating an agent's behaviour, we must take these restrictions into account. But even then the predictability of her behaviour cannot be a given. The amount of information she possesses and her perception of the strategy restrictions in place, makes accurate prediction of her behaviour unlikely. The homo economicus model of neoclassical economics is an approximation and simplification of human behaviour and as such it can only be used under certain conditions for the construction of theoretical models. Therefore, a more plausible account of human behaviour would have to relax some of the strict assumptions of economic rationality. Moreover, the proposed account of rationality within bounds considers the fact that human agents live in social groups and as such are bound to interact repetitively.

Rationality and maximisation depend primarily on the agent's perception of available strategies and environmental limitations, which in turn depend on available information. Thus, rational agents acting in the same environment should adopt similar strategies. There is no full information in this respect, but there is access to roughly equal information. Each rational agent has access to the same amount of information and therefore should adopt the same strategy in order to maximise her utility. Rational individuals with access to similar information should make similar decisions and adopt similar strategies. This does not assume that preferences have to converge for a convention to be formed; rather it refers to a common understanding of the principles of social interactions. Individuals do not have to have similar preferences and it is likely that they will have conflicting interests. However, equal rationality should lead to a decision making process that leads to an optimal outcome. Put differently, there is equal rationality within a social group or convention, as opposed to the neoclassical models which assume equal rationality for all.

Furthermore, it is realistic to assert that each agent has roughly the same memory. It does not have to be full memory of every decision in the game's history, but "each individual remembers a general experience of the game but not how he fared against particular opponents" (Sugden, 2004: 60), so that each player has a general understanding of how agents with whom he has interacted behave. And this understanding creates a disposition to act accordingly in the future. If the player has interacted mostly with cooperators (or he believes he has), then it is more likely he will expect his future interactions to be with cooperators.

7 Ethics, justice and profit

The theoretical argument of the previous five chapters has implications for real world interactions. Economic phenomena such as boycotting, the shared economy and micro-finance achieve economic success as well as moral outcomes. Moreover, there are other areas of economic activity such as labour relations, financial and supra-national corporations and the food industry, where the ethical dimension of supply and distribution have been the focus of attention and public debate. Economics as an ethical theory shows that efficiency in economic terms must correspond to ideas of justice as mutual advantage and that profit maximising behaviour corresponds to moral behaviour. In order for this argument to hold then we need to revisit the idea of free markets and capitalism and qualify it to be closer to a mutual advantage capitalism. This is an alternative approach to contemporary free market capitalism and addresses contemporary anti-capitalistic criticism. The financial crisis of 2008 for example was the result of individuals and corporations maximising profit at the expense of their customers and society as a whole, taking advantage of information and power asymmetries. Chapter 2 argued for an understanding of economics that incorporates moral, economic and social behaviour, whereas modern capitalism relies on keeping these realms separate. At the same time, the argument presented here is one for freedom of markets, which relies on freedom of individuals and personal responsibility. Repeated interactions between informed, rational individuals lead to social equilibria that are efficient and moral. Individual freedom and responsibility, as well as the sustainability and efficiency of social equilibria all rely on information availability, within a given society.

Theoretically, information availability, and even information equality, is ensured by the assumption of repeated interactions. As interaction history develops within a social group or society, its members develop a better understanding of how potential interlocutors are likely to behave in the future, using past behaviour as basis for prediction. Practically, this is not as straightforward; however, information today is much more easily spread than a few years ago thanks to technological advancements. Assuming access to the internet for instance, it is plausible to assert that all consumers have access to the same information about a certain product. It is then their personal responsibility to decide whether they should consume it. For example, everyone has the capacity to know whether an investment portfolio relies on high risk investments, which food is organic, a given bank executives' salaries. It is up to the individual consumer to decide whether she ought to consume the given product. As such, information symmetries in the market place are more plausible today than even before, mostly because of advancements in information technology. They are not always present, information symmetries in the sense of information equality within the bounds of a society is a possibility and present in many cases. As a result, social equilibria that regulate and promote moral behaviour, as discussed in earlier chapters, can become established. In this context, social equilibria that call for risky investments or industrially produced food can also become established, but they cannot be as efficient as equilibria that rely on long-term sustainability.

An inclusive social contract

Contractarian ethics revolves around the issue of who is owed moral consideration and is to be considered a moral agent. For many contractarians, only contributors to the social contract are to be included in the contract whereas for others, reasoning ability is the base-point. This is especially relevant to economic theory which in its most basic form only includes economic agents, producers and consumers. Non-contributors, or non-active economic agents, can be included in the social contract. Non-contributors can be distinguished into two categories: willing, rational non-contributors and those who cannot reason or lack the ability to contribute. The latter case can include those who are severely handicapped, but it can also include animals interactions with whom cannot be reciprocal. However, they can be part of a moral social contract in the sense that they can be the object of moral considerations. They can be treated by contractors as means, rather than ends in themselves. This allows rational agency to be the second requirement for the proposed moral contract. Economic agents 'use' non-contributors to promote their utility. Indirect reciprocity allows for rational, selfish agents to interact with non-contributors, as long as they interact in an environment of repeated interactions and information availability. Interactions with or behaviour towards non-contributors is seen as a way to promote one's reputation as a moral agent, thus increasing one's potential for interactions leading to moral outcomes. This approach fits especially well with the book theme as it allows to link self-interested maximisation with moral consideration.

Contractarian ethics postulate that ethics is the result of agreement between rational agents. John Rawls (2003) argues that rational agents should reach an agreement about social ethics, should they consider themselves outside society and behind a veil of ignorance. Behind the veil of ignorance rational individuals will agree on impartial and fair rules regulating social behaviour, since they are aware of their social position and as such can be objective about potential social situations and in a sense empathetic. Rawls's work established contractarianism as the basis of contemporary political philosophy and as such for many of the current debates on ethics, and especially animal ethics (Svolba, 2016). David Gauthier (1986) following in the contractarian tradition argues that rational, self-interested individuals have reasons to agree on the rules of a social contract dictating moral behaviour and justice. Gauthier's argument relies on a series of provisions about the original position and agents' reasoning capacities. He argues that rational, mutually unconcerned agents agree to cooperate in a prisoner's dilemma game, should they find themselves interacting with similarly disposed interlocutors. Thus, they exhibit other-regarding behaviour despite being selfish utility maximisers. However, both of their arguments can be reinforced by accepting that rational deliberation is influence by social circumstances. Economic agents, individuals or corporations, are self-interested and mutually unconcerned, primarily aiming at utility maximisation. However, this maximisation takes place within a social context, which makes their behaviour known. If one does not mistreat animals, for instance, one might be rewarded by those who believe that animals should not be mistreated. In a social contract where this is not acceptable behaviour, mistreating animals would be irrational. As such behaviour is dictated by maximisation opportunities rather than empathy or other non-rational considerations. That leaves the argument open to criticism, as morality depends on the established social equilibrium. Indirect reciprocity might serve as a mechanism for replicating irrational and immoral, as well as rational and moral, behaviour. However, having assumed repeated interactions and rational agency, we can expect that agents prefer a cooperative to a noncooperative social equilibrium since the former allows for higher utility over time (Binmore, 2007). As such, it is more likely that a cooperative equilibrium that maximises social welfare will be as inclusive as possible, thus making animal mistreatment immoral. Again, the account of social morality derives its forces from its roots in rationality rather than its immediate and universal effect. Social development can take time and develop over generations. As a result, the moral equilibrium is the result of improvements over generations.

More practically, reputation is especially relevant to businesses that want to 'advertise' their behaviour. Over time, it pays for businesses to incorporate any financial costs that moral behaviour towards animals might entail in their maximisation function. This is true in social equilibria where mistreating animals is at least frowned upon. A business can 'advertise' its moral behaviour towards animals to attract customers who care about animals. At the same time customers who do not care about animal welfare would select an interlocutor with moral past over one whose past interactions have yielded lower utility as a result of a defection equilibrium. However, given that cooperative societies achieve higher utility for their members that non-cooperative ones, it pays for businesses to 'advertise' moral behaviour towards animals even in societies where mistreating animals is acceptable. It is more likely that an agent who behaves morally with animals will behave morally with humans and as such, this agent will be able to participate in more cooperative interactions. In conclusion, deriving the account of social morality presented here from rational premises is especially appropriate to economic and business ethics, given that firms are rational agents operating for profit.

The individual and the social contract

The fundamental cornerstone of each social group and society is the social contract. The following paragraphs will attempt to examine to what degree the assumed interdependence of the social contract and social conventions, and the central role of individual action, make sense in the real world.

In the discussion in this and the previous chapters, the social contract is seen as consisting of social conventions that arise from repeated interactions. At the same time, social structures define and bound rational agents' strategy sets and social behaviour. Therefore, there is a bi-directional relationship between social structures, namely social conventions and the social contract, and individual action. A change in the social contract has to occur through a gradual change in its social conventions in order to be sustained. Thus, the social contract is seen as the equilibrium in a repeated game which is reached only when its sub-games have reached their respective topical equilibria.

A shift in the social equilibrium will not necessarily cause all the sub-game equilibria to collapse, especially when they are stable. However, for a social contract to shift to a new stable equilibrium, most of its component social conventions will have to reach new stable social equilibria; the co-evolution of the social contract and its conventions does not require the collapse of either, but it can be achieved as an adjustment to the existing rules of behaviour (Diamond, 1997; Diamond, 2000; Tainter, 1988). Cultural evolution can explain how social contracts came about and why they are stable, but it does not include an analysis of their optimisation (Young, 2001) since, in the evolutionary analysis, an equilibrium can be evolutionarily stable but not optimal. Equilibrium optimality depends on the optimality of the constitutive social conventions. In turn, social conventions depend on individual behaviour. Rationality in interactions can cause equilibria to shift towards more efficient or optimal states.

Conventions such as driving on the left cannot change over an election cycle or even a generation, when they have been established for centuries. Of course, the driving convention is only an over-simplified convention that does not affect social welfare. More important and more deeply rooted conventions are more complicated structurally and so more difficult to shift. For instance, the imposition of democracy in societies without a democratic culture will not lead to a democratic state or a society with democratic values; democracy depends on a multitude of institutions and behaviours throughout society and the political realm, and a third party imposition that requires drastic convention change in short periods cannot be effective. Holding an election when there is not a social culture of democratic principles, or in other words established topical conventions that are not democratic, cannot make a society democratic.

This poses questions about the level of change individual behaviour can cause. However, given the accelerated time of cultural evolution and information spreading that is possible nowadays, it is realistic to assert that a local convention can bring about change at a social contract level within reasonable time. For instance, in many parts of Africa female genital mutilation was an established convention until recently, despite social and economic progress and a rise in literacy. This changed after a small number of villages decided collectively to abandon the practice, which triggered the change in several other village clusters, to the point that it became illegal in Senegal only a year after the first village meeting (Bowles in Salvadori, 2010). Rational individuals can cause large scale change by establishing higher utility social conventions in their local interactions.

Rational actors within conventions have been assumed to be allowed to behave according to their rational deliberation even if that leads them to non-conventional strategies. This makes evolution of conventions and the process by which a society reaches higher welfare states possible. For this to be achieved, freedom of individual action and absence of coercion are essential so as that rational agents can use all the information available to them, learn from their own past and adapt to environmental changes, in order to make maximising decisions. Agents who behave non-conventionally are punished by exclusion but any other authoritative form of behaviour enforcement would mean that the evolutionary process would be skewed. It is imperative to keep in mind that cultural evolution includes errors and therefore, irrational behaviour and non-optimal equilibria are useful as lessons of what to avoid in the future and also as a method to try new strategies that might prove more efficient. Learning through trial and error applies both to rational agents and social conventions and in order to have an evolutionary process of social conventions it is vital that individuals experiment and make errors. Therefore, individual behaviour does affect the evolution of conventions and indirectly the evolution of the social contract. Individual rational strategies evolve in parallel with the evolution of the social contract.

The question of how one ought to act relates, in the context presented here, to the issue of whether individual action can influence social structures or society determines individual behaviour. The essence of the question is whether an individual has any real power over collective decisions and more importantly over social structures and their evolution. To an extent, Karl Marx was right to claim that man makes his own history in predefined circumstances (Hollis, 1994). If the social contract consists of social conventions that rational agents should follow, then it might seem there is little room for personal responsibility and individual rationality once these conventions are established. However, the social contract through social conventions is dynamic and individual behaviour can cause change on a social level. The individual has the responsibility to be rational through adaptation, imitation and learning (Young, 2001).

A further problem with the realism of this account of individual action within a society that is described by social conventions is the presence of extreme inequalities. Even though the stability of the social contract is not necessarily threatened, extreme inequalities as well as the use of coercion threaten its cohesion and optimality. Information symmetries level the field to a degree but in real life there are significant inequalities within a society, or in other words among members of the same social contract. When there are extreme inequalities – as is often the case in the real world – rational interactions become impossible and therefore there is a need for formal institutions to regulate interactions. Any institution whose purpose would be to reduce those inequalities would therefore have to provide the means for equal access to information and ensure inter-conventional discrepancies do not increase inequalities. In that respect, institutions are required to facilitate information spreading and to ameliorate extreme inequalities, especially between conventions.

Interactions among rational utility maximisers should lead to commonly accepted outcomes that are Pareto efficient, but this is not always the case, especially when there are information discrepancies that make rational deliberation reach different outcomes. There are, in this sense, discrepancies in rational deliberation outcomes which nullify the assumptions of equal bounded rationality and rational utility maximisers. In these cases, there is a need for a third party that addresses issues of incompatibility between social conventions. The more homogeneous a society, the less the need for a third party enforcer, for instance in a society where social conventions have converged so that rational interactions are possible does not need an external enforcer. However, this only occurs locally and within conventions. Social conventions that are homogeneous enough to ensure acceptance of the status-quo or agreement on any deviation are more plausible.

Social institutions are in themselves conventions and are bound by the same rules as lower level conventions like the driving game. Therefore, any type of institution that has evolved without external enforcement will ensure the best available results in terms of social welfare within the specific environmental parameters. Administrative and legal institutions have evolved in similar ways as the driving conventions. Therefore, they cannot be changed arbitrarily, without underlying conventions shifting as well. Social conventions that define cultural norms affect formal conventions such as the government and the legal system. Hence, they are supportive of the formal institutions and they have to shift before any institutional change becomes realistic.

The convergence of social conventions and individual rationality may very well lead to consensus over important to matters. This is a direct implication of asserting that rationality can be common to all and given the same information rational agents will reach the same conclusions. This not always empirically true. Rational individuals with access to the same information often make different decisions. Therefore, convergence of individual behaviour is not always a given.

In a world of competing conventions and individual behaviour, it is easier to argue that there can be an evolutionary process of convention and behaviour convergence. Societies with different historical backgrounds choose different conventions of social behaviour. One cannot change the past but one has to adapt to it in the best possible way. A maximising strategy is maximising given a specific environment and in diverse environments there will be different maximising strategies. Absence of coercion means that one culture cannot enforce specific equilibria on others using universal moral laws as justification. Each convention ought to reach an optimal equilibrium through its own specific historical evolution. Therefore, there is not much point or need to discuss an optimal social contract. There can be more than one optimal social contract, given that optimality depends on the underlying conventions. Different conventions support different social contracts and imitating more successful social contracts without the appropriate conventions cannot be sustainable. On this view the social contract cannot be seen as a mechanism for social peace that should be designed for optimality. Although it is apparent that "mechanism design is based on the obvious principle that decision-making should be decentralized to the people who have the necessary knowledge and experience" (Binmore, 2005: 136), deciding who those people are depends on the values of each society.

Top-down or bottom-up accounts of social and individual behaviour (Hollis, 1994), are therefore misplaced. One has to take into account a complementary view of co-evolution of social structures and individual behaviour for an accurate description of how human societies and individuals within them, operate.

Social rationality in the real world

Real world societies are at equilibria which might be of various types, but individuals within these societies know what kind of behaviour the equilibrium requires of them. A person can have certain expectations of others and also has a rough memory of how she fared against specific other individuals; "when in Rome do like the Romans do". Those who do not in the conventional account of social interactions can be traced and excluded from social interactions (Andrés Guzmán et al., 2007). Rational agents conform to established social conventions and norms since their rational strategies have co-evolved with the dynamics of the existing social structures (Skyrms, 2004). A single visitor in Rome may be involved in one-off interactions and may be indifferent to the prospect of being excluded. In this sense, there are two groups: the Romans and the visitors. If many visitors perceive their interactions as one-off interactions, where cooperation is irrational, the Romans will behave accordingly. Then, Rome will develop a reputation as being hostile towards strangers, and over time there will be fewer visitors, harming both groups.

In an idealised model of the world, one's behaviour would become known and punished either in Rome or in one's native convention. In the real world this is not as easily achieved. However, it is plausible to assert that lone exploiters, visitors who break local conventions, can be punished even within the limited scope of their visit. Provided that they will interact with the local population, punishment is possible. For instance, a visitor to a foreign country who litters might not be fined or the fine might be insignificant, but he can expect lack of cooperation from the natives next time he asks for information. Therefore, by littering, agents do not maximise their utility even for short-term interactions given there is information about their actions.

Interactions are to be seen as repeated since individuals act within a given convention where there are established norms of behaviour and communication of information and there is information about their interactions outside the convention. The repetitiveness of interactions means that all interactions can be described as games where joint strategies yield higher utility to all players. For example, in the Prisoner's Dilemma (PD) game, when both prisoners know that they will interact again in the same environment, they will coordinate their behaviour so as to maximise their utility. Whether this is still a PD game or not, in the formal sense, is not important. What matters in this context is that it more accurately describes rational interactions. Repeated interactions and the capability of agents to learn and remember, within reason, show that an account of bounded rationality is more plausible and effective in describing rational behaviour. In addition, the above understanding of game theory as a descriptive tool of social interactions gives an account of existing social structures that are cooperative and a result of having adopted joint and not individual strategies.

The account of bounded rationality that has been used to support the concept of rational conventions, as opposed to economic rationality, is not unrealistic. People learn from their experiences and they want to maximise their benefit as often as possible. Moreover, it is common and expected that the same people interact more than once; it is more realistic to claim that individuals encounter each other in repeated interactions than not. People live in societies, towns and neighbours and therefore, it is much more likely that most of their interactions will be with their neighbours and people living in the same town, than with people living in a different country. At the same time low individual rationality does not necessarily lead to sub-optimal equilibria (Young, 2001). Assumptions of rational agents with near complete information are usually seen as idealised assumptions; however, through recent technological developments full information has become a more plausible assumption. Furthermore, it is reasonable to assert that most people within a convention have access to the same information and that information spreads quickly within the bounds of the given convention.

A social convention is bound and formed by information availability, a common conception of maximising behaviour, and a general common understanding of how social problems can be resolved. It is in a sense tautological to say that within a convention agents have access to similar information and similar rational capabilities. If they did not, the convention would not have formed in the first place. Similar accounts of rationality lead to similar deliberative outcomes about how to maximise individual utility. For instance, some conventions may call for maximisation through debate while others through force; in the former case intellectual skills are needed, whereas in the latter physical power is required. In both conventions, despite their fundamental differences, there is a common understanding of how to maximise. And within the limits of each convention, it is rational to behave conventionally. Therefore, if we take the existence of social conventions as a given, the assumption of agents with similar capabilities to reason and access to similar information, is anything but an idealised assumption.

Bounded or conventional rationality and economic rationality are identical in that agents are assumed to be mutually unconcerned utility maximisers. However, conventional rationality does not require complete memory, infinite processing power, or a capacity to predict the future with high degrees of accuracy. Hence, the conventional account of rationality is closer to the way real humans reason. In fact, including mutual unconcern in bounded rationality may be seen as an unnecessary addition since individuals are not always mutually unconcerned; they develop bonds and behave in ways that are frequently not explained by rational choice theory. In reality humans care for family and friends without a need for constraints on their rationality. Most humans are not always mutually unconcerned with respect to any person with whom they interact, which at least sometimes makes them behave irrationally according to the economic account of rationality, which requires that a rational agent should maximise her utility irrespective of whom she interacts with or other environmental parameters. Assuming that they are mutually unconcerned however, means that moral responsibilities deriving from an assumption of mutual unconcern will also include interactions between agents who are mutually concerned. Offering an account of rationality based incentives for moral behaviour can only strengthen the argument presented here. Therefore, in a realistic setting mutual unconcern, although not always present in interactions, does not threaten the assumption of rational agency.

An individual has to be rational, which means that she has to stay open to receiving new information and actively seek new knowledge about the possibilities of conventional maximisation. A rational conventional agent has to be ready to be critical of her convention should there be a rational justification for doing so. At the same time a rational agent who has accepted the rationality of her convention has to behave conventionally other things being equal. Put differently, a rational agent ought to behave rationally. This sounds tautological and superfluous but there is a need for a type of active rationality. Conventional rationality demands that agents use their assumed rationality to confirm that they are part of a rational, utility maximising convention. This thinking creates explicit normative obligations for conventional agents. Realistically, one cannot continue behaving in the same way when those around have shifted to a new behavioural pattern. In the real world people behave in a certain way only if it pays; should they realise that their behaviour is no longer maximising they change it. For instance, a rational committed party voter will only continue voting if the party's political positions remain similar to hers. If either her or the party's positions change, she will also change her voting behaviour. This is not always the case, but it seems reasonable to assert that it is the case more often than not and whenever is not, it merely shows how conventions influence rational behaviour.

Conventional behaviour is plausible and can describe rational behaviour with high degrees of accuracy. However, there are several problems when we try to apply conventional accounts of rationality to the real world. First of all, although it is plausible to say that everyone living in a region or within a social group has access to the same information, this is not a sufficient condition for maximisation. Individuals choose to make use of some pieces of information and to ignore others. Using different information, both in terms of quality and quantity, results in adopting different strategies. Although the information processing power in all adult humans can be said to be roughly the same, some people are better at it. Thus there are inequalities arising from the ability to use the available information efficiently. Moreover, in the real world information is often expensive and/or not widely available. Again, those who can afford it or know where to find it have an advantage in interactions. In this context, therefore, the discrepancy between the real world and the theory lies on information availability. It is plausible to assert that information is rather readily available, especially since the creation and development of the internet, but real life experience shows that to be less than accurate.

Another, closely related, assumption that can be criticised as idealistic, is the ability of individuals and groups to learn. Long-established conventions resist change and people within those conventions are more likely than not to prefer a status-quo that is not Pareto optimal than the uncertainty of change. Accounts of conventional rationality can deal with these problems. Rationality is viewed at the level of social convention, where information is roughly similar, learning is easier and trying new strategies is not irreversible. Therefore the realism of the assumptions of bounded rationality is related to the realism of the assumptions of social conventions which will be discussed next.

An appropriate example of how a social rationality analysis can be used in a real world case is the Rwanda genocide in 1994. Farming land in Rwanda had been expanding for decades. People continued doing what maximised their and previous generations' utility in the past; therefore it was rational to try to farm on as much land as possible. This in turn led to a population increase up to the point where the land could not support so many people. Since more land was becoming available through methods like deforestation, there was no rational incentive for farmers to modernise or try new crops (Diamond, 2011).

Farmers in Rwanda during the 1980s were behaving rationally, both as individuals and a society. Within the limitations of conventional rationality this outcome could not be foreseen. Even if scientists in Rwanda had all the data available and could predict that there would be a Malthusian food crisis, it would have been extremely difficult for them to predict the genocide. Despite the fact that crises like the 1994 one had occurred before in Rwanda, they were limited by comparison and usually attributed to tribal competition and local culture rather than an over-exploitation of natural resources and lack of economic and social planning (ibid). People in Rwanda were being boundedly rational within the limitations of the available information and knowledge. Based on the history of interactions and the rules of the established convention, foreseeing the catastrophe was realistically impossible.

A boundedly rational agent could have analysed the situation and reached a useful conclusion – at least it seems so after the effect. Previous violent outbursts as a result of land and food shortages were not considered serious enough to convince people who had been farming for generations on the same lands using similar methods that their tried and tested lifestyle would lead to a genocide. As discussed previously, the longer a social convention has been established for and the more successful it has been, the more difficult it is to change. Successful farming and population growth were controlled by local, non-catastrophic violence that included redistributing land and reducing the population. The 1994 genocide was the peak of a series of smaller scale violent events stemming from the same roots.

These factors created a relative indifference to violence that was seen as a cultural or racist phenomenon unrelated to individuals' living standards. A rational agent in pre-1994 Rwanda would have to constrain his maximisation; live off smaller areas of land and follow family planning principles. This case exhibits how conventional rationality can define individual preferences and limit agents' freedom to act. Moreover, it shows that great inequalities within a social contract have to be dealt with through a third party. Furthermore, cynically speaking the genocide itself can be seen as an evolutionary step. The overpopulation was controlled, land was redistributed and the violence had such a great effect on the local culture as to ensure that future similar events will be avoided by a better informed and more knowledgeable population.

Usually in the real world, the case with established social conventions is that they have been active over many generations and therefore it is more difficult for a single rational agent to have accurate information and to reason adequately about individual and social maximisation. Incremental change over long periods of time is very difficult, if not impossible, to detect and poses significant problems to rational agents trying to understand their environment. Looking at historic societies can offer significant insights into the behaviour of social conventions and rational agents.

Easter Island had a complex society and culture before being first visited by European explorers in the second half of the 18th century. However, by the time of the first contact with Europeans, Easter Island inhabitants had been reduced in number and their society was in decay. Archaeological evidence indicates that the famous Easter Island monuments were erected at a time of affluence for religious purposes. The island had rich forests that provided timber that made building such monuments possible while supporting a healthy economy and society. A combination of specific climatic conditions and human behaviour led to the almost complete deforestation of Easter Island by the end of the 18th century. Rational or even reasonable people should have been able to adjust their behaviour to the changing physical environment of the island. Deforestation has to have taken place over several generations and its devastating outcomes must have been apparent at some point before all the trees of the island were extinguished. The same applies of course in the case of human intervention. If we accept that deforestation was a result of the islanders' over-consumption, we have to question their inability to be even marginally prudent. Easter Island's climate is more fragile by comparison to similar islands and therefore, more sensitive to human activity. The physical climate is not as interesting for this discussion as Easter Islanders' response to a changing environment; or rather the lack of response.

Most archaeological evidence suggests that the Easter Island statues were erected to exhibit political power or as religious symbols (ibid). At the time of their construction they promoted social cohesion and peace while showing off the local chief's power. In that respect they were essential. The islanders' religious and social culture required these sculptures to continue being built even when it became apparent that it was becoming unsustainable in terms of resources. The motives for building monuments became so socially entrenched that they overpowered rational calculation. A political and religious system that had become so successful and long-lived would pose problems to rational sceptics. The gradual deforestation and its incremental effects on social life were not powerful enough factors to cause social change, before the lack of trees enforced that change and lead to decay (ibid).

The Easter Island geographical isolation created more problems as the local society could not have asked for outside help or discovered information about more successful social conventions that they could then imitate. Just as in the case of Rwanda, the Easter Island society failed to adapt to a changing environment. What was rational originally became catastrophic as social structures failed to evolve and the physical environment could not sustain the same behaviour. Although it might seem that the physical environment was central to the Easter Island case, that is not true. The physical resources of the island as well as its isolation played a role, but the important factor was that the local society failed to perceive that social changes were needed; and that failure to evolve culturally had to do first and foremost with the structure of the given society and only then its physical environment.

The above cases of Rwanda and Easter Island show how rational agents ought to take into account historical evidence, learn about similar societies and adapt to environmental changes in order to maximise. The same principles apply to successful social conventions. Preserving conventional behaviour can be destructive or productive, depending on an accurate understanding of the environment. It becomes obvious then that accurate information and data, as well as communication, are paramount for the adoption of rational strategies. Given that human rational capabilities cannot change significantly, a rational agent and a rational convention must take into account as many parameters as possible in order to sustain maximisation.

Both in Rwanda and Easter Island, "human activities dramatically altered the environment, and this in turn changed the course of cultural evolution" (Ehrlich, 2002). Both these examples focus on the environmental impact of human behaviour and on how societies fail to adapt to a changing physical environment. However, they also apply as realistic paradigms of how rational agents and sustainable social conventions need to continue evaluating their behaviour in order to remain rational. An agent must take into account her social and physical environment in order to be rational. If changes in the environment occur, it might very well be rational at a given time to follow strategies that several years or decades later would be catastrophically irrational. Moreover, these examples show how information availability is essential for rationality and also poses the problem of evolutionary time.

Even in cultural evolution environmental changes occur slowly by comparison to the duration of a human life and, just as in biological evolution, social conventions change over several generations (Boyd and Richerson, 1988). The problems of evolutionary time in political and moral philosophy and the realism of information availability will be discussed in the following paragraphs, where there will be special emphasis on the changes in the establishment and stability of social conventions caused by technological advancements. The next section will discuss how the assumption of equal information and information availability is more realistic in the contemporary world than it used to be and how that affects the possibility of equal rationality.

Information symmetry and the economy

The ease of information spreading in the contemporary world shows knowledge of a plethora of social conventions and social contracts, a fact that would have been impossible without the technological advancements of the past couple of centuries. Being able to travel further in the 19th and 20th centuries as well the availability of more accurate information in the last 100 years, gives us the capability to compare and contrast our conventions with those in every other part of the world. This ability creates responsibilities from a rational choice perspective; if we find out about more efficient equilibria we ought to imitate the behaviour observed there. In the same spirit, if western developed societies have a moral obligation to help those in need anywhere in the world, it is because of the mere fact that today more than ever before they know about their situation and they have the ability to change it (Barry, 1991). Similarly, the internet and the possibilities it has created for communication and learning have profound implications for political philosophy and the assumption of rationality.

Information availability is a realistic assumption in the contemporary world and has significant effects on our understanding of personal responsibility. An agent can learn which is the maximising behaviour in a given environment and which social conventions maximise social welfare. The more the internet becomes part of social life the more diverse information becomes easily available and the closer societies get to being societies of fully, or at least equally, informed individuals. Moreover, the body-mind separation (Matthews in Hoven and Weckert, 2009), makes it more plausible to assert that there can be societies where physical skills are not linked to contribution to the cooperative surplus. It is plausible to argue then that the information age brings us closer to a society of individuals with roughly equal capabilities. The expansion of information technologies and the fact that they have become more easily accessible to more people creates an equality of information availability, which can lead to agents of roughly equal rational capabilities. Equal rationality ensures rational, mutually beneficial interactions and subsequently efficient social conventions.

The account of economic rationality is probably only observed in the real world in corporative behaviour. Corporations and businesses keep detailed records of their past performance and use all the means at their disposal to accurately predict the future. Agents of bounded rationality may not have the detailed and accurate account of their past or the predictive means that companies do. However, just like companies, all agents within a convention have access to roughly the same amounts of information. Therefore, using their rational capabilities, they can make decisions in the same framework. If there could be an argument for a for-profit business to constrain its maximisation, it would also apply to rational actor models. The following subsection will look some real world cases were businesses decided to constrain their maximisation as a method of maximising their profits.

Freemium is a successful business model where paying for the product is, in a sense, voluntary since many, if not a majority of consumers, do not pay (Pujol, 2010). Some consumers, usually businesses and professionals, can select to pay for more advanced services and thus, make it possible for freemium companies to give away their product to those who are not willing to pay (Bekkelund, 2011). Free-riders in this model are welcome in that they help the company advertise its product and expand – they serve as cooperators with apparent dispositions. This model is primarily seen in companies that are active on the internet (such as Dropbox), but there is no reason for it to be limited there. As long as there is a service or a product it is easy to see how constraining maximisation is profitable in economic terms. The same applies for more traditional consumables, although it is not as straightforward. Free samples have been an established advertising practice for many years (Pujol, 2010). It is not too far-fetched to say that there can be companies that will offer a proportion of their product at prices that are very low or even below production, so as to increase their consumer base. A typical case is low-cost airlines that sell some tickets at very low prices, provided there is a form of cooperation by consumers, such as booking long in advance or waive some services. Despite restrictions such as the need for low marginal costs and a relatively long-lived and large consumer base, some freemium companies have shown that it is possible to be as competitive as traditionally organised companies.

However, the relative success of business models like freemium does not mean that traditional businesses cannot be equally or more profitable. Word of mouth effects that are vital for freemium companies also apply to traditional companies. However and more importantly, the freemium model shows that it is viable for a for-profit company to give away small quantities of its product and to make profit from large consumers only. Inequalities are embedded in the model and the weak – those using the product for free – are essential for the company's profits, since they are used as advertisers. Having a good reputation is essential since information spreading (i.e. free advertisement) as well as the number of paying customers depend on the quality of the product. Since it is safe to assume that only rational individuals will use or buy the product, there will be a strictly mutually advantageous relationship with the company. The vulnerable, the non-paying consumers, are vital for information spreading which makes the model viable.

Similar principles apply to all economic transactions as information availability creates individual responsibility. Micro-financing was made possible to a large extent because of the possibility of informing poorer people about the prospects and the benefits of their cooperation (Vatta, 2003). The relative success of micro-finance exhibits how extreme power inequalities do not always make rational interactions impossible. The weak can form groups, or conventions, in order to interact with those much stronger. In this light we can claim that there are economic models that inform moral conventions of cooperation and constrained maximisation. Therefore, at least within some economic models, there is room for embedded principles of fairness.

A fair price in contemporary societies and economies is one that is determined by the free market mechanism. A market mechanism that works more efficiently will produce prices that meet the fairness criterion. In order for this to happen, full or at least equal information is essential for both buyers and sellers. Information for both products and sellers and buyers has to be freely available, in order to be used for assessment in future interactions. Just as reputations matter in repeated games within social conventions, in an ideal market past interactions count towards a seller's or buyer's reputation and determine success or failure. This is even more likely in today's information age where the availability of information is easier and cheaper; for instance, eBay can store seller's and buyer's ratings for all their transactions, which are then used as an accurate indication of their behaviour (Cohen, 2003).

An ideally competitive market is indeed a morally free-zone (Gauthier, 1986); there is no need for moral values or principles to be introduced in order for the market to lead to moral outcomes. Rather, the morality of the market depends on the ability of economic agents to behave rationally, within the context of sociability and intertemporality.

The morality of free market

Contractarian ethics is ideally suited to discuss ethics in free markets and capitalism because they share rational agency as starting point. Individual responsibility and freedom are requirements for both systems. However, capitalism does not always lead to moral outcomes – or rather it very rarely does. Both propositions are theoretical but capitalism and its outcomes are everyday reality.

Contemporary capitalism is characterised by extreme power inequalities, which originate in wealth and property ownership inequalities and translate into information inequalities that reinforce them. As such, considering that the current state of affairs is the starting point or the original position in the social contract, the power of the individual is significantly reduced. That said, the significance of rational agency has important effects on the idea of personal responsibility and by extension consumer responsibility. An interaction between a multinational firm and a consumer is one-sided, but consumers can avoid interactions with much more powerful agents to avoid being taken advantage. Furthermore, as it was discussed in Chapters 3–5, agents must avoid such interactions as a consequence of their rational agency. Individual agents then have the option to only interact with smaller firms and more realistically, to interact as a group of consumers. This is not merely consumer organisation or consumer rights but rather rationality-based free market at work. Going back to the animal mistreatment example, consumers who care about it must avoid firms that mistreat animals. Given information availability, such information can be made available – especially today with the advancement of information technology. Similar principles apply to any other topic such as for example employee working conditions. If rational agents/consumers care about such an issue, they have rational obligation to avoid interaction with the firm. In time, such behaviour will shift the social and economic equilibrium towards one that is more in line with the majority's rational deliberation outcomes. In practice, such rational behaviour of avoiding interactions with much more powerful agents are observed in cases such as micro-finance (Vatta, 2003), where collective action is adopted to address power discrepancies and the so-called political consumerism. Both of these types of behaviour have been successful in interactions with more powerful agents, usually corporations. Especially political consumerism can be achieved through spread of information and with minimal levels of formal organisation.

Political consumerism, buycotting and boycotting (Kam and Deichert, 2020) are the ideas the individuals consider ethical issues before consuming. It is linked to the premises of moral contractarianism as presented here. This allows to suggest that when boycotting is rational it is also moral. Organisations and individuals are participants in the same social contract and boycotting is a form of social exclusion. Defectors, organisations and individuals who do not adhere to the rules of the established social contract, are excluded from social interactions. The basis for exclusion is rational morality; agents have rational reasons to boycott and exclusion is shown to be moral. Consumers as a social group have more power than individual consumers, and as a result they can shift the social equilibrium that allows practices such as animal mistreatment, or any practice that is not deemed acceptable.

The social contract is a mechanism for the establishment and enforcement of rules of social and moral behaviour. It is based on the implicit or explicit consent of the participants and it aims at mutual advantage. Participants are responsible for following the rules that have been agreed upon through participation in social life and for punishing defectors. Behaviour that is not in line with the rules of the contract must be punished in order to preserve the contract. Enforcement lies on the contracting parties as well as enforcement mechanisms. In the economic marketplace, boycotting firms that do not adhere to the provisions of the established or aspired social contract is a rational imperative. The force of the argument lies on its liberal premises; the stability of the established economic social contract depends on the individuals' consent (Murray, 2007).

Boycotting itself has been viewed as withdrawal of cooperation (Smith, 2014) and as such in contractarian terms it can be seen as social exclusion. So boycotting in a contractarian framework is about two things. First, it is about choosing one's interlocutors based on past behaviour. This includes abstention from consumption of certain goods and services thus excluding the respective organisations offering these goods and services. Second and complementary, boycotting is about the accountability of all parties in the contract, including corporations and organisations. If they are boycotted, they fail to maximise and therefore, they have reasons to be included in the established social contract.

An important issue that arises from this approach is power inequalities. Great power discrepancies between interlocutors can make mutually advantageous interactions impossible, given there is no third party enforcer. Practically this applies to interactions between organisations and individuals and the impact of boycotting. This issue is dealt with by referring to the effect of interaction abstention by large numbers of individuals as well as by powerful agents, or else organisations, who do not want to be associated with defectors.

The proposed contractarian approach to boycotting reinforces the argument about boycotting on two levels: First, it emphasises and explains the importance of individual action and small groups. Second, it offers a deeper analytical framework for the theoretical premises and implications of boycotting that considers social dynamics as well as self-interest. Boycotting is about individual maximisation as well as social welfare. Therefore, there is no need for relying on arguments about morality since boycotting is shown to be rational. Moral contractarianism assumes and requires rational individuals for a moral social contract and the same is shown to be true for successful boycotting.

References

Andrés Guzmán, R., Rodríguez-Sickert, C., Rowthorn, R., 2007. When in Rome, Do as the Romans Do: The Co-evolution of Altruistic Punishment, Conformist Learning, and Cooperation. *Evolution and Human Behavior* 28, 112–117. doi:10.1016/j.evolhumbehav.2006.08.002

Barry, B., 1991. *Theories of Justice*. University of California Press, Oakland.

Bekkelund, K.J., 2011. Succeeding with Freemium: Exploring Why Companies Have Succeeded and Failed with Freemium. *Innovation and Entrepreneurship*, Specialization Project 4350, 6–7.

Bergstrom, T.C., 2002. Evolution of Social Behavior: Individual and Group Selection. *The Journal of Economic Perspectives* 16, 67–88.

Bicchieri, C., 2002. *The Grammar of Society: The Nature and Dynamics of Social Norms*. Cambridge University Press, New York.

Binmore, K., 1998. *Game Theory and the Social Contract: Just Playing v. 2.* MIT Press.

Binmore, K., 2007. *Playing for Real: A Text on Game Theory*. Oxford University Press.

Binmore, K., 2005. *Natural Justice*. Oxford University Press, Oxford.

Binmore, K., 1989. Social Contract I: Harsanyi and Rawls. *The Economic Journal* 99, 84–102.

Bloom, P., 2018. *Against Empathy: The Case for Rational Compassion*. Vintage, London.

Bowles, S., Gintis, H., 2013. *A Cooperative Species: Human Reciprocity and Its Evolution*, Reprint edition. Princeton University Press, Princeton.

Boyd, R., Richerson, P.J., 1988. *Culture and the Evolutionary Process*. University of Chicago Press., Chicago.

Braithwaite, R.B., 1955. *Theory of Games as a Tool for the Moral Philosopher*, 1st ed. Cambridge University Press, New York.

Broome, J., 1999. *Ethics Out of Economics*. Cambridge University Press, Cambridge.

Cohen, A., 2003. *The Perfect Store: Inside EBay*, New ed. Piatkus, Boston.

Coleman, J.L., Morris, C.W., 1998. *Rational Commitment and Social Justice: Essays for Gregory Kavka*. Cambridge University Press, Cambridge.

Cudd, A., 2007. Contractarianism [WWW Document]. URL http://plato. stanford.edu/entries/contractarianism/#3 (accessed 11.24.10).

Dawkins, R., 2006. *The Selfish Gene.* Oxford University Press, Oxford.

Diamond, J., 2000. How to Organize a Rich and Successful Group: Lessons from Natural Experiments in History. *Bulletin of the American Academy of Arts and Sciences* 53, 20–33. doi:10.2307/3824806

Diamond, J., 1997. Location, Location, Location: The First Farmers. *Science,* New Series 278, 1243–1244.

Diamond, J., 2011. *Collapse: How Societies Choose to Fail or Survive.* Penguin, London.

Dimock, S., 2010. Defending Non-Tuism. *Canadian Journal of Philosophy* 29, 251–273.

Durant, W., 2010. *The Lessons of History.* Simon & Schuster, New York.

Ehrlich, P.R., 2002. *Human Natures: Genes, Cultures, and the Human Prospect,* Reissue. ed. Penguin Putnam, London.

Elster, J., 1985. Rationality, Morality, and Collective Action. *Ethics* 96, 136–155.

Elster, J., 1982. The Case for Methodological Individualism. *Theory and Society* 11, 453–482.

Forst, R., 2002. *Contexts of Justice: Political Philosophy beyond Liberalism and Communitarianism.* University of California Press, Berkeley.

Frank, R.H., 1988. *Passions within Reason: The Strategic Role of Emotions,* 1st ed. W W Norton & Co Inc, New York.

Gaus, G.F., 2011. *The Order of Public Reason: A Theory of Freedom and Morality in a Diverse and Bounded World.* Cambridge University Press, Cambridge.

Gaus, G., 2013. Why the Conventionalist Needs the Social Contract (and Vice Versa). Special Topic: Can the Social Contract Be Signed by an Invisible Hand? *Rationality, Markets and Morals* 4, 71–87.

Gauthier, D., 2013. Twenty-Five On. *Ethics* 123, 601–624. doi:10.1086/670246

Gauthier, D., 1986. *Morals by Agreement.* Clarendon Press, Oxford.

Gauthier, D., 1979. David Hume, Contractarian. *The Philosophical Review* 88, 3–38.

Gauthier, D., Sugden, R. (Eds.), 1993. *Rationality, Justice and the Social Contract: Themes from "Morals by Agreement."* The University of Michigan Press, Ann Arbor.

Gigerenzer, G., 2002. *Bounded Rationality: The Adaptive Toolbox,* New ed. MIT Press, Cambridge, MA.

Gintis, H., 2009. *The Bounds of Reason: Game Theory and the Unification of the Behavioral Sciences.* Princeton University Press, New Jersey.

Gintis, H., 2006. *Moral Sentiments and Material Interests: The Foundation of Cooperation in Economic Life,* New ed. MIT Press, Cambridge, MA.

Grapard, U., Hewitson, G., 2012. *Robinson Crusoe's Economic Man: A Construction and Deconstruction.* Routledge, London.

Haakonssen, K., 2006. *The Cambridge Companion to Adam Smith.* Cambridge University Press, Cambridge; New York.

Hampton, J., 1988. Hobbes and the Social Contract Tradition, New Ed. Cambridge University Press, Cambridge; New York.

Hardin, G., 1968. The Tragedy of the Commons. *Science*, New Series 162, 1243–1248.

Hargreaves–Heap, 1989. *Rationality in Economics*. Wiley-Blackwell, New York.

Hargreaves-Heap, 2004. *Game Theory: A Critical Introduction*. Routledge, London.

Hartogh, G.D., 1993. The Rationality of Conditional Cooperation. *Erkenntnis* (1975-) 38, 405–427.

Hausman, D.M., 1989. Are Markets Morally Free Zones? *Philosophy & Public Affairs* 18, 317–333.

Heath, J., 2015. Methodological Individualism [WWW Document]. The Stanford Encyclopedia of Philosophy. https://plato.stanford.edu/archives/spr2015/entries/methodological-individualism/ (accessed 3.17.20).

Heilbroner, R., 1986. The Nature and Logic of Capitalism, New ed. W. W. Norton & Company, New York.

Hobbes, T., 1976. *Leviathan*. Forgotten Books, London.

Hofbauer, J., Sigmund, K., 1998. *Evolutionary Games and Population Dynamics*. Cambridge University Press, Cambridge.

Hollis, M., 1975. *Rational Economic Man: A Philosophical Critique of Neo-classical Economics/Martin Hollis [and] Edward J. Nell*. Cambridge University Press, London.

Hollis, M., 1994. *The Philosophy of Social Science: An Introduction*. Cambridge University Press, Cambridge.

Hoven, J. van den, Weckert, J. (Eds.), 2009. *Information Technology and Moral Philosophy*, 1st ed. Cambridge University Press, Cambridge.

Hume, D., 1985. *A Treatise of Human Nature*. Penguin Classics, London.

Kam, C.D., Deichert, M., 2020. Boycotting, Buycotting, and the Psychology of Political Consumerism. *The Journal of Politics* 82, 72–88. https://doi.org/10.1086/705922

Katz, L.D. (Ed.), 2000. *Evolutionary Origins of Morality: Cross Disciplinary Perspectives*. Imprint Academic, Thorverton, UK; Bowling Green, OH.

Kavka, G.S., 1983. The Toxin Puzzle. *Analysis* 43, 33–36. doi:10.2307/3327802

Kymlicka, W., 1990. *Contemporary Political Philosophy: An Introduction*. Clarendon Press, Oxford.

Leinfellner, W., Köhler, E. (Eds.), 1998. *Game Theory, Experience, Rationality: Foundations of Social Sciences, Economics and Ethics in honor of John C. Harsanyi*, 1998 edition. ed. Springer, Dordrecht.

Levin, J., 2010. Functionalism [WWW Document]. The Stanford Encyclopedia of Philosophy. http://plato.stanford.edu/archives/sum2010/entries/functionalism/ (accessed 8.27.12).

Martin, M., McIntyre, L.C., 1994. *Readings in the Philosophy of Social Science*. MIT Press, Cambridge, MA; London.

Matravers, M., 2000. *Justice and Punishment: The Rationale of Coercion*. Oxford University Press, Oxford.

McClennen, E.F., 1990. *Rationality and Dynamic Choice: Foundational Explorations*. Cambridge University Press, Cambridge.

Morris, C.W., Ripstein, A., 2001. *Practical Rationality and Preference: Essays for David Gauthier*. Cambridge University Press, Cambridge.

Murray, M., 2007. *The Moral Wager: Evolution and Contract*, 1st ed. Springer, Dordrecht.

Murray, M. (Ed.), 2007. *Liberty, Games and Contracts: Jan Narveson and the Defence of Libertarianism*. Ashgate Publishing, Ltd, Aldershot, England.

Narveson, J., Dimock, S., 2000. *Liberalism: New Essays on Liberal Themes*. Springer, Dordrecht.

Nida-Rümelin, J., Spohn, W., 2000. *Rationality, Rules, and Structure*. Springer, Dordrecht.

North, D.C., 1991. Institutions. *The Journal of Economic Perspectives* 5, 97–112.

Ostrom, E., 2000. Collective Action and the Evolution of Social Norms. *The Journal of Economic Perspectives* 14, 137–158.

Parfit, D., 1986. *Reasons and Persons*, New Ed. Oxford University Press, New York.

Pujol, N., 2010. *Freemium: Attributes of an Emerging Business Model*. SSRN eLibrary.

Rawls, J., 2005. *A Theory of Justice*. Harvard University Press, Cambridge, MA.

Rawls, J., 2003. *Justice as Fairness: A Restatement*. Harvard University Press, Cambridge, MA.

Reich, R., 2017. *Saving Capitalism: For the Many, Not the Few*. Icon Books Ltd, London.

Rescorla, M., 2011. Convention [WWW Document]. The Stanford Encyclopedia of Philosophy. http://plato.stanford.edu/archives/spr2011/entries/convention/ (accessed 8.28.12).

Rosling, H., Rosling, O., Rönnlund, A.R., 2019. *Factfulness: Ten Reasons We're Wrong About The World – And Why Things Are Better Than You Think*, 01 edition. ed. Sceptre, London.

Salvadori, N. (Ed.), 2010. *Institutional and Social Dynamics of Growth and Distribution*. Edward Elgar Publishing Ltd, Cheltenham, UK; Northampton, MA.

Sandel, M., 2012. *What Money Can't Buy: The Moral Limits of Markets*. Allen Lane, London; New York.

Schelling, T.C., 2006. *Micromotives and Macrobehavior*. Norton, New York.

Sen, A., 1988. *On Ethics and Economics*. New ed. Wiley-Blackwell, Oxford.

Sen, A., 2009. *The Idea of Justice*. Harvard University Press, Cambridge, MA.

Skyrms, B., 2010. *Signals: Evolution, Learning, and Information*. Oxford University Press, Oxford.

Skyrms, B., 2004. *The Stag Hunt and the Evolution of Social Structure*. Cambridge University Press, Cambridge.

Smith, A., Haakonssen, K., 2002. *The Theory of Moral Sentiments.* Cambridge University Press, Cambridge.

Smith, N.C., 2014. *Morality and the Market (Routledge Revivals): Consumer Pressure for Corporate Accountability.* Routledge, London.

Sugden, R., 2004. *The Economics of Rights, Co-operation, and Welfare.* Palgrave Macmillan, London.

Svolba, D., 2016. Is There a Rawlsian Argument for Animal Rights? *Ethical Theory and Moral Practice* 19, 973–984. https://doi.org/10.1007/s10677-016-9702-0

Tainter, J.A., 1988. *The Collapse of Complex Societies, New Studies in Archaeology.* Cambridge University Press, Cambridge; Cambridgeshire; New York.

Taylor, M., 1987. *The Possibility of Cooperation.* Cambridge University Press, Cambridge.

Vallentyne, P. (Ed.), 1991. *Contractarianism and Rational Choice: Essays on David Gauthier's Morals by Agreement.* Cambridge University Press, New York.

Vanderschraaf, P., 1999. Game Theory, Evolution, and Justice. *Philosophy & Public Affairs* 28, 325–358.

Vanderschraaf, P., 2011. Justice as Mutual Advantage and the Vulnerable. *Politics, Philosophy & Economics* 10, 119–147. doi:10.1177/1470594X10386566

Vatta, K., 2003. Microfinance and Poverty Alleviation. *Economic and Political Weekly* 38, 432–433.

Verbeek, B., 2002. *Instrumental Rationality and Moral Philosophy: An Essay on the Virtues of Cooperation.* Springer, Dordrecht.

Weirich, P., 2011. Exclusion from the Social Contract. *Politics, Philosophy & Economics* 10, 148–169. doi:10.1177/1470594X10387262.

Young, H.P., 2001. *Individual Strategy and Social Structure.* Princeton University Press, New Jersey.

Index

Printed in the United States
by Baker & Taylor Publisher Services